Neo4j Data Modeling

Steve Hoberman

David Fauth

Align > Refine > Design Series

Technics Publications

Published by:

115 Linda Vista, Sedona, AZ 86336 USA
https://www.TechnicsPub.com

Edited by Sadie Hoberman
Cover design by Lorena Molinari
Illustrations by Joseph Shepherd

First Printing 2023
Copyright © 2023 by Technics Publications

ISBN, print ed.	9781634621915
ISBN, Kindle ed.	9781634621922
ISBN, ePub ed.	9781634621939
ISBN, PDF ed.	9781634621960

Library of Congress Control Number: 2023933990

Contents

About the Book

My daughter can make a mean brownie. She starts with a store-bought brownie mix and adds chocolate chips, apple cider vinegar, and other "secret" ingredients to make her own unique delicious brownie.

Building a robust database design meeting users' needs requires a similar approach. The store-bought brownie mix represents a proven recipe for success. Likewise, there are data modeling practices that we have proven successful over many decades. The chocolate chips and other secret ingredients represent the special additions that lead to an exceptional product. Neo4j has a number of special design considerations, much like the chocolate chips. Combining proven data modeling practices with Neo4j design-specific practices creates a series of data models representing powerful communication tools, greatly improving the opportunities for an exceptional design and application.

In fact, each book in the Align > Refine > Design series covers conceptual, logical, and physical data modeling for a specific database product, combining the best of data modeling practices with solution-specific design considerations. It is a winning combination.

My daughter's first few brownies were not a success, although as the proud (and hungry) dad, I ate them anyway—and they were still pretty tasty. It took practice to get the brownie to come out amazing. We need practice on the modeling side as well. Therefore, each book in the series follows the same animal shelter case study, allowing you to see the modeling techniques applied to reinforce your learning.

If you are interested in learning how to build multiple database solutions, read all the books in the series. Once you read one, you'll be able to pick up the techniques for another database solution even quicker.

Some say my first word was "data". I have been a data modeler for over 30 years and have taught variations of my **Data Modeling Master Class** since 1992—currently up to the 10th Edition! I have written nine books on data modeling, including *The Rosedata Stone* and *Data Modeling Made Simple*. I review data models using my Data Model Scorecard® technique. I am the founder of the Design Challenges group, creator of the Data Modeling Institute's Data Modeling Certification exam, Conference Chair of the Data Modeling Zone conferences, director of Technics Publications, lecturer at Columbia University, and recipient of the Data Administration Management Association (DAMA) International Professional Achievement Award.

Thinking of my daughter's brownie analogy, I have perfected the store-bought brownie recipe. That is, I know how to model. However, I am not an expert in every database solution.

That is why each book in this series combines my proven data modeling practices with a database solution expert. So for this book, Dave Fauth and I are building the brownie together. I work on the store-bought brownie piece, and he works on adding the chocolate chips and other delicious ingredients. Dave is a Neo4j thought leader. Here is more about Dave:

I have been working with Neo4j and graph databases since about 2012. Graphs are a natural extension of the way we think so the technology was fascinating. Since joining Neo4j in 2014, I have worked with customers implementing Neo4j to address their business needs. A successful Neo4j deployment starts with a data model that will help address a business' most pressing questions.

We hope our tag team approach shows you how to model any Neo4j solution.

We wrote this book for two audiences:

- Data architects and modelers who need to expand their modeling skills to include Neo4j. That is, those of us who know how to make a store-bought brownie but are looking for those secret additions like chocolate chips.

- Database administrators and developers who know Neo4j but need to expand their modeling skills. That is, those of us who know the value of chocolate chips and other ingredients, but need to learn how to combine these ingredients with those store-bought brownie mixes.

This book contains a foundational introduction followed by three approach-driven chapters. Think of the introduction as making that store-built brownie and the subsequent chapters as adding chocolate chips and other yummy ingredients. More on these four sections:

- **Introduction: About Data Models.** This overview covers the three modeling characteristics of precise, minimal, and visual; the three model components of entities, relationships, and attributes; the three model levels of conceptual (align), logical (refine), and physical (design); and the three modeling perspectives of relational, dimensional, and query. By the end of this introduction, you will know data modeling concepts and how to approach any data modeling assignment. This introduction will be useful to database administrators and developers who need a foundation in data modeling, as well as data architects and data modelers who need a modeling refresher.

- **Chapter 1: Align.** This chapter will explain the data modeling align phase. We explain the purpose of aligning our business vocabulary, introduce our animal shelter case study, and then walk through the align approach. This chapter will be useful for both audiences, architects/modelers and database administrators/developers.

- **Chapter 2: Refine.** This chapter will explain the data modeling refine phase. We explain the purpose of refine, refine the model for our animal shelter case study, and then walk through the refine approach.

This chapter will be useful for both audiences, architects/modelers and database administrators/developers.

- **Chapter 3: Design**. This chapter will explain the data modeling design phase. We explain the purpose of design, design the model for our animal shelter case study, and then walk through the design approach. This chapter will be useful for both audiences, architects/modelers and database administrators/developers.

We end each chapter with three tips and three takeaways. We aim to write as concisely yet comprehensively as possible to make the most of your time.

Most data models throughout the book were created using Hackolade Studio (https://hackolade.com) and are accessible for reference at https://github.com/hackolade/books along with additional sample data models to play with.

Let's begin!

Steve and Dave

About Data Models

This chapter is all about making that store-built brownie. We present the data modeling principles and concepts within a single chapter. In addition to explaining the data model, this chapter covers the three modeling characteristics of precise, minimal, and visual; the three model components of entities, relationships, and attributes; the three model levels of conceptual (align), logical (refine), and physical (design); and the three modeling perspectives of relational, dimensional, and query. By the end of this chapter, you will know how to approach any data modeling assignment.

Data model explanation

A model is a precise representation of a landscape. Precise means there is only one way to read a model—it is not ambiguous nor up to interpretation. You and I read the same model the exact same way, making the model an extremely valuable communication tool. We need to 'speak' a language before we can discuss content. That is, once we know how to read the symbols on a model (syntax), we can discuss what the symbols represent (semantics).

Once we understand the syntax, we can discuss the semantics.

For example, a map helps a visitor navigate a city. Once we know what the symbols mean on a map, such as lines representing streets and blue representing water, we can read the map and use it as a valuable navigation tool for understanding a geographical landscape.

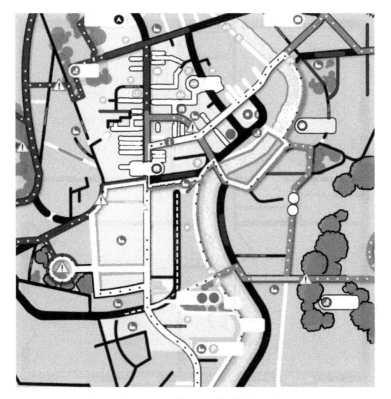

Figure I-1: Map of a geographic landscape.

A blueprint helps an architect communicate building plans. The blueprint, too, contains only representations, such as rectangles for rooms and lines for pipes. Once we know what the rectangles and lines mean on a blueprint, we know what the structure will look like and can understand the architectural landscape.

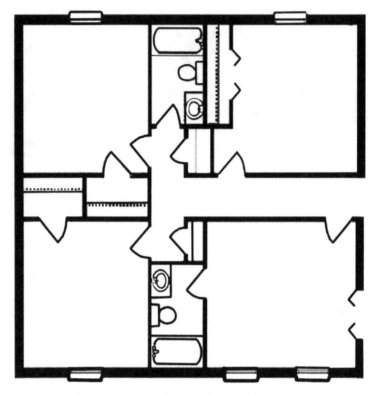

Figure I-2: Map of an architectural landscape.

A data model helps business and IT professionals communicate the business vocabulary and business requirements for a particular initiative. The data model, too, contains only representations, such as rectangles for business terms and lines capturing the reasons these terms interact with each other. Once we know what the rectangles and lines mean on a data model, we can debate and eventually agree on the vocabulary and requirements for an initiative. That is, we can understand a particular informational landscape.

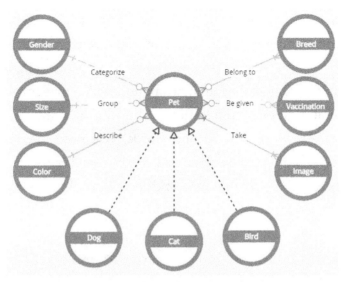

Figure I-3: Map of an informational landscape.

A data model is a precise representation of an information landscape. We build data models to confirm and document our understanding of other perspectives.

In addition to precision, two other important characteristics of the model are minimal and visual. Let's discuss all three characteristics.

Three model characteristics

Models are valuable because they are precise—there is only one way to interpret the symbols on the model. We must transform the ambiguity in our verbal and sometimes written communication into a precise language. Precision does not mean complex—we need to keep our language simple and show the minimal amount needed for successful communication. In addition, following the maxim "a picture is worth a thousand words," we need visuals to communicate this precise and simple language for the initiative. Precise, minimal, and visual are three essential characteristics of the model.

Precise

Bob: How's your course going?

Mary: Going well. But my students are complaining about too much homework. They tell me they have many other classes.

Bob: The attendees in my advanced session say the same thing.

Mary: I wouldn't expect that from graduates. Anyway, how many other offerings are you teaching this semester?

Bob: I'm teaching five offerings this term and one is an evening not-for-credit class.

We can let this conversation continue for a few pages, but do you see the ambiguity caused by this simple dialog?

- What is the difference between **Course, Class, Offering,** and **Session?**
- Are **Semester** and **Term** the same?
- Are **Student** and **Attendee** the same?

Precision means "exactly or sharply defined or stated." Precision means there is only one interpretation for a term, including the term's name, definition, and connections to other terms. Most issues organizations face related to growth, credibility, and saving lives, stem from a lack of precision.

On a recent project, Steve needed to explain data modeling to a group of senior human resource executives. These very high-level managers lead departments responsible for implementing a very expensive global employee expense system. Steve felt the last thing these busy human resource executives needed was a lecture on data modeling. So instead, he asked each of these managers sitting around this large boardroom table to write down their definition of an employee. After a few minutes, most of the writing stopped and he asked them to share their definitions of an employee.

As expected, no two definitions were the same. For example, one manager included contingency workers in his definition, while another included summer interns. Instead of spending the remaining meeting time attempting to come to a consensus on the meaning of an employee, we discussed the reasons we create data models, including the value of precision. Steve explained that after we complete the difficult journey of achieving the agreed-upon employee definition and document it in the form of a data model, no one will ever have to go through the same painful process again. Instead, they can use and build upon the existing model, adding even more value for the organization.

Making terms precise is hard work. We need to transform the ambiguity in our verbal and sometimes written communication into a form where five people can read about the term and each gets a single clear picture of the term, not five different interpretations. For example, a group of business users initially define **Product** as:

Something we produce intending to sell for profit.

Is this definition precise? If you and I read this definition, are we each clear on what *something* means? Is *something* tangible like a hammer or instead some type of service? If it is a hammer and we donate this hammer to a not-for-profit organization, is it still a hammer? After all, we didn't make a *profit* on it. The word *intending* may cover us, but still, shouldn't this word be explained in more detail? And who is *we*? Is it our entire organization or maybe just a subset? What does *profit* really mean anyway? Can two people read the word *profit* and see it very differently?

You see the problem. We need to think like a detective to find gaps and ambiguous statements in the text to make terms precise. After some debate, we update our **Product** definition to:

A product, also known as a finished product, is something that is in a state to be sold to a consumer. It has completed the manufacturing process, contains a wrapper, and is labeled for resale. A product is different than a raw material and a semi-finished good. A raw material, such as sugar or milk, and a semi-finished good, such as melted chocolate, is never sold to a consumer. If, in the future, sugar or milk is sold directly to consumers, then sugar and milk become products.

Examples:
Widgets Dark Chocolate 42 oz
Lemonizer 10 oz
Blueberry pickle juice 24 oz

Ask at least five people to see if they are all clear on this particular initiative's definition of a product. The best way to test precision is to try to break the definition. Think of lots of examples and see if everyone makes the same decision as to whether the examples are products or not.

In 1967, G.H. Mealy wrote a white paper where he made this statement:

> We do not, it seems, have a very clear and commonly agreed upon set of notions about data—either what they are, how they should be fed and cared for, or their relation to the design of programming languages and operating systems.[1]

Although Mr. Mealy made this claim over 50 years ago, if we replace *programming languages and operating systems* with the word *databases*, we can make a similar claim today.

Aiming for precision can help us better understand our business terms and business requirements.

Minimal

The world around us is full of obstacles that can overwhelm our senses and make it very challenging to focus only on the relevant information needed to make intelligent decisions. Therefore, the model contains a small set of symbols and text, simplifying a subset of the real world by only including representations of what we need to understand. Much is filtered out on a model, creating an incomplete but extremely useful reflection of reality. For example, we might need to communicate the descriptive information

---

1 G. H. Mealy, "Another Look at Data," AFIPS, pp. 525-534, 1967 Proceedings of the Fall Joint Computer Conference, 1967. http://tw.rpi.edu/media/2013/11/11/134fa/GHMealy-1967-FJCC-p525.pdf.

about **Customer**, such as their name, birth date, and email address. But we will not include information on the process of adding or deleting a customer.

Visual

Visual means that we need a picture instead of lots of text. Our brains process images 60,000 times faster than text, and 90 percent of the information transmitted to the brain is visual.[2]

We might read an entire document but not reach that moment of clarity until we see a figure or picture summarizing everything. Imagine writing a document to navigate from one city to another versus having a map describe visually how the roads connect.

Three model components

The three components of a data model are entities, relationships, and attributes (including keys).

---

[2] https://www.t-sciences.com/news/humans-process-visual-data-better.

Entities

An entity is a collection of information about something important to the business. It is a noun considered basic and critical to your audience for a particular initiative. Basic means this entity is mentioned frequently in conversations while discussing the initiative. Critical means the initiative would be very different or non-existent without this entity.

The majority of entities are easy to identify and include nouns that are common across industries, such as **Customer**, **Employee**, and **Product**. Entities can have different names and meanings within departments, organizations, or industries based on audience and initiative (scope). An airline may call a **Customer** a *Passenger*, a hospital may call a **Customer** a *Patient*, and an insurance company may call a **Customer** a *Policyholder*, yet they are all recipients of goods or services.

Each entity fits into one of six categories: who, what, when, where, why, or how. That is, each entity is either a who, what, when, where, why, or how. Table I-1 contains a definition of each of these categories, along with examples.

The term *entity* is broad and independent of technology. For example, an entity in Oracle is a *table* or *view*. An entity in MongoDB is a *collection*. An individual entity in Neo4j is called a *node*, while a set of entities are grouped together using a *label*.

Category	Definition	Examples
Who	Person or organization of interest to the initiative.	Employee, Patient, Player, Suspect, Customer, Vendor, Student, Passenger, Competitor, Author
What	Product or service of interest to the initiative. What the organization makes or provides that keeps it in business.	Product, Service, Raw Material, Finished Good, Course, Song, Photograph, Tax Preparation, Policy, Breed
When	Calendar or time interval of interest to the initiative.	Schedule, Semester, Fiscal Period, Duration
Where	Location of interest to the initiative. Location can refer to actual places as well as electronic places.	Employee Home Address, Distribution Point, Customer Website
Why	Event or transaction of interest to the initiative.	Order, Return, Complaint, Withdrawal, Payment, Trade, Claim
How	Documentation of the event of interest to the initiative. Records events such as a Purchase Order (a "How") recording an Order event (a "Why"). A document provides evidence that an event took place.	Invoice, Contract, Agreement, Purchase Order, Speeding Ticket, Packing Slip, Trade Confirmation

Table I-1: Entity categories plus examples.

A quick aside on graphs…

Graphs and graph databases store the relationships between the entities within their data. The relationships between the entities are considered as important as the entities themselves. This allows users to traverse the data based on the relationship types in the data and identify paths, patterns (normal or abnormal), communities, points of failure, and many other analytical uses. Graphs allow businesses to join a variety of datasets and run these analytics at scale.

Graph databases like Neo4j store nodes and relationships instead of tables or documents. Data is stored just like you might sketch ideas on a whiteboard. Your data is stored without restricting it to a pre-defined model, allowing a very flexible way of thinking about and using it.

Since the data is *joined* when the data is stored, these traversal queries can be run in sub-seconds instead of hours and days. The database does not need to continually join data together to identify the patterns allowing businesses to make sense of their data.

In the example in Figure I-4, a business may want to make a fraud detection graph. The graph will consist of entities and their identifiers such as Social Security Number, Email, and Phone Number. Once the graph is created, queries can be run to identify users sharing identifiers. Users can also run community detection algorithms to identify fraud rings.

Neo4j is a Labeled Property Graph (LPG). A Labeled Property Graph is a type of graph database. In an LPG database, the graph is comprised of nodes and relationships. A node is an instance of an entity. A relationship provides directed, named, connections between two nodes. Both nodes and relationships can have properties that describe the node or relationship.

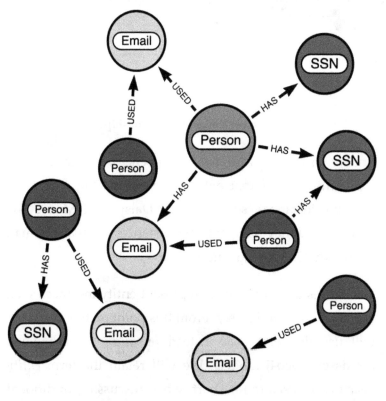

Figure I-4: Fraud detection graph.

Neo4j uses labels to shape the domain by grouping (classifying) nodes into sets where all nodes with a certain label belong to the same set. A label is equivalent to an entity. From this point on this book, we will use the term *label* instead of *entity* when discussing Neo4j models. We will retain the term *entity* when discussing traditional data models.

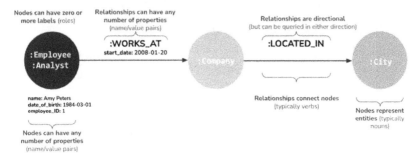

Figure I-5: Nodes and relationships.

Entity instances are the occurrences, examples, or representatives of that entity. The entity **Dog** may have multiple instances, such as Spot, Daisy, and Misty. The entity **Breed** may have multiple instances, such as German Shephard, Greyhound, and Beagle.

Neo4j uses the term *node* to represent entity instances such as Spot, Daisy, and Misty. From this point on this book, we will use the term *node* instead of *entity instance* when discussing Neo4j models. We will retain the term *entity instance,* or *instance* for short, when discussing traditional data models.

For example, in our initiative, we may have multiple individual pets (such as Spot, Daisy, and Misty) that we would assign the label **Pet**. We would do the same for the various breeds, such as Poodle, Boxer, Terrier, and assign them the label **Breed**. On a traditional data model, entities appear as rectangles, such as these two for our animal shelter:

Figure I-6: Traditional entities.

On Neo4j's LPG data model, we are going to model sets of individual entities and assign them a label. The set of entities will be shown as circles in our data model and are identified by a label name. In Neo4j, our **Pet** and **Breed** entities would look like the following:

Figure I-7: Labels in Neo4j.

An entity instance can belong to more than one entity. For example, Bob Jones can be an **Employee**, a **Student**, or a **Consumer**. Bob Jones can also be an example of the generic **Person** entity.

In a relational database like Oracle, Bob Jones would be replicated in potentially four different tables (**Person, Employee, Student, Consumer**) or Bob Jones would have different columns to indicate their entity type within the

Person table. In Neo4j, we can assign the individual Bob Jones node multiple labels, such as **Employee, Student, Consumer**, and **Person**. There is only a single individual node, but the node contains multiple labels.

Figure I-8: A node can contain multiple labels.

For data modeling purposes, it might be easier for business users to understand this if represented as a subclass:

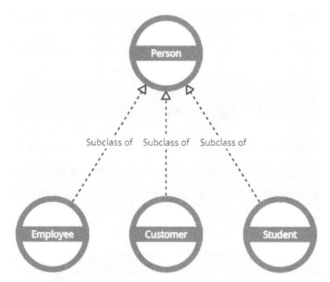

Figure I-9: A multi-label node with subclasses.

Relationships

A relationship captures the verb connecting two nouns. A relationship connects two nouns represented as two entities in a traditional data model. A relationship connects two nouns represented as two nodes in Neo4j.

In Neo4j, a relationship exists between two individual nodes. There is no implied inheritance. If we have a set of nodes with a **Pet** label and a set of nodes with a **Breed** label, not every individual **Pet** must have a relationship to a node with the **Breed** label. We may not know the **Breed** for our **Pet** named Boots. Figure I-10 shows the model that may occur.

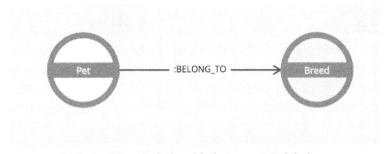

Figure I-10: A relationship between two labels.

Since the relationship is between individual nodes and Neo4j does not support that the relationship must exist between labels, we may see **Pets** with no **Breed** and a **Breed** with no **Pets**.

As a best practice, we will model the relationships between labels and not model based on individual data elements. For example, Figure I-11 shows a relationship between **Pet** and **Breed**.

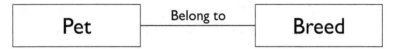

Figure I-11: A traditional relationship between Pet and Breed.

The phrase **Belong to** is called a *verb phrase*. A verb phrase adds meaning to the relationship. Instead of just saying that a **Pet** may relate to a **Breed**, we can say that a **Pet** may belong to a **Breed**. **Belong to** is more meaningful than **Relate**.

So far, we know that a relationship represents a business connection between two entities. It would be nice to know more about the relationship, such as whether a **Pet** may belong to more than one **Breed** or whether a **Breed** can categorize more than one **Pet**. Enter cardinality.

Cardinality means the additional symbols on the relationship line that communicate how many instances from one entity participate in the relationship with instances of the other entity.

There are several modeling notations, and each notation has its own set of symbols. Throughout this book, we use a notation called *Information Engineering (IE)*. The IE notation has been a very popular notation since the early 1980s. If you use a notation other than IE within your organization, you must translate the following symbols into the corresponding symbols in your modeling notation.

We can choose any combination of zero, one, or many for cardinality. *Many* (some people use "more") means one or more. Yes, many includes one. Specifying one or many allows us to capture *how many* of a particular entity instance participate in a given relationship. Specifying zero or one allows us to capture whether an entity instance is or is not required in a relationship.

Recall this relationship between **Pet** and **Breed**:

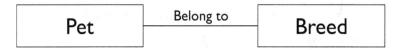

Figure I-12: A traditional relationship between Pet and Breed.

Let's now add cardinality. We first ask the *Participation* questions to learn more. Participation questions tell us whether the relationship is 'one' or 'many'. So, for example:

- Can a **Pet** belong to more than one **Breed**?
- Can a **Breed** categorize more than one **Pet**?

A simple spreadsheet can keep track of these questions and their answers:

Question	Yes	No
Can a Pet belong to more than one Breed?		
Can a Breed categorize more than one Pet?		

We asked the animal shelter experts and received these answers:

Question	Yes	No
Can a Pet belong to more than one Breed?	✓	
Can a Breed categorize more than one Pet?	✓	

We learn that a **Pet** may belong to more than one **Breed**. For example, Daisy is part Beagle and part Terrier. We also learned that a **Breed** may categorize more than one **Pet**. Both Sparky and Spot are Greyhounds.

'Many' (meaning one or more) on a data model in the IE notation is a symbol that looks like a crow's foot (and is called a *crow's foot* by data folks). See Figure I-13.

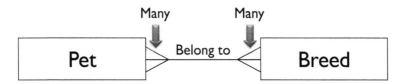

Figure I-13: Displaying the answers to the Participation questions.

Now we know more about the relationship:

- Each **Pet** may belong to many **Breeds**.
- Each **Breed** may categorize many **Pets**.

We also always use the word 'each' when reading a relationship and start with the entity that makes the most sense to the reader, usually the one with the clearest relationship label.

This relationship is not yet precise, though. So, in addition to asking these two Participation questions, we also need to ask the *Existence* questions. Existence tells us for each relationship whether one entity can exist without the other term. For example:

- Can a **Pet** exist without a **Breed**?
- Can a **Breed** exist without a **Pet**?

We asked the animal shelter experts and received these answers:

Question	Yes	No
Can a Pet exist without a Breed?		✓
Can a Breed exist without a Pet?	✓	

So, we learn that a **Pet** cannot exist without a **Breed**, and that a **Breed** can exist without a **Pet**. This means, for example, that we may not have any Chihuahuas in our animal shelter. Yet we need to capture a **Breed** (and in this case, one or more **Breeds**), for every **Pet**. As soon as we know about Daisy, we need to identify at least one of her breeds, such as Beagle or Terrier.

Figure I-14 displays the answers to these two questions.

After adding existence, we have a precise relationship:

- Each **Pet** must belong to many **Breeds**.
- Each **Breed** may categorize many **Pets**.

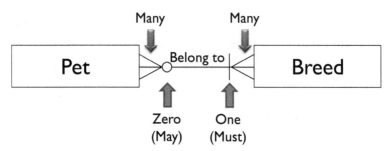

Figure I-14: Displaying the answers to the Existence questions.

The Existence questions are also known as the May/Must questions. The Existence questions tell us when reading the relationship, whether we say "may" or "must." A zero means "may", indicating optionality—the entity can exist without the other entity. A **Breed** *may* exist without a **Pet**, for example. A one means "must", indicating required—the entity cannot exist without the other entity. A **Pet** *must* belong to at least one **Breed**, for example.

There are two more questions that need to be asked, if we are working at the more detailed logical data model (which will be discussed shortly). These are the *Identification* questions.

Identification tells us for each relationship whether one entity can be identified without the other term. For example:

- Can a **Pet** be identified without a **Breed**?
- Can a **Breed** be identified without a **Pet**?

We asked the animal shelter experts and received these answers:

Question	Yes	No
Can a Pet be identified without a Breed?	✓	
Can a Breed be identified without a Pet?	✓	

So, we learn that a **Pet** can be identified without knowing a **Breed**. We can identify the pet Sparky without knowing that Sparky is a German Shepherd. In addition, we can identify a **Breed** without knowing the **Pet**. This means, for example, that we can identify the Chihuahua breed without including any information from **Pet**.

A dotted line captures a non-identifying relationship. That is, when the answer to both questions is "yes". A solid line captures an identifying relationship., That is, when one of the answers is "no".

Non-identifying

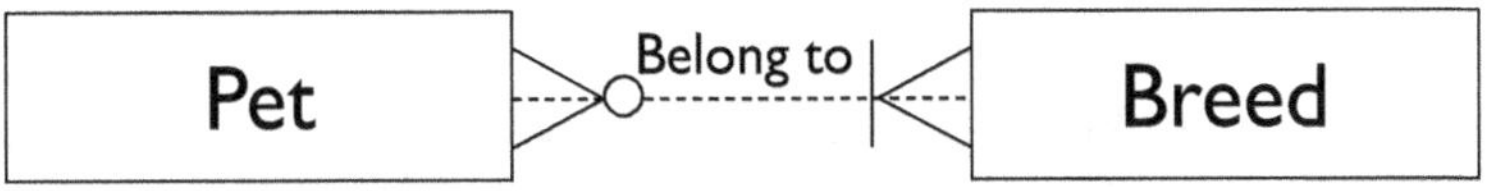

Identifying

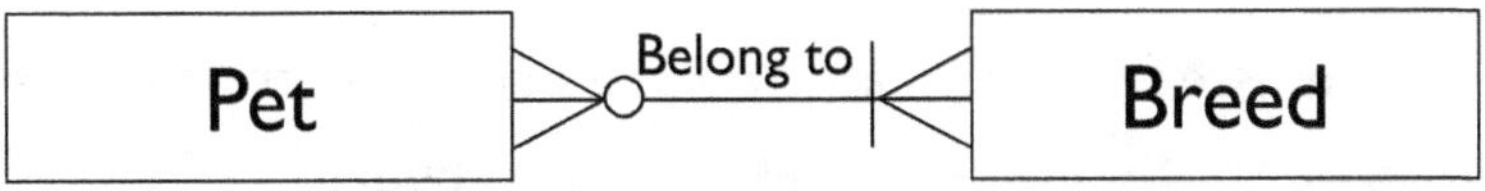

Figure I-15: A non-identifying (top) and identifying (bottom) relationship.

So, to summarize, the Participation questions reveal whether each entity has a one or many relationship to the other entity. The Existence questions reveal whether each entity has an optional ("may") or mandatory ("must") relationship to the other entity. The Identification questions reveal whether each entity requires the other entity to bring back a unique entity instance.

Use instances to make things clear in the beginning and eventually help you explain your models to colleagues. See Figure I-16 for an example.

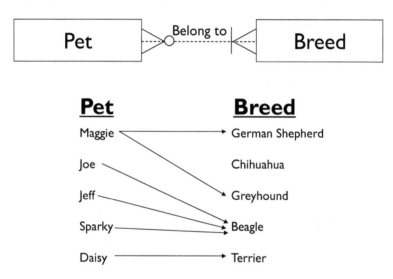

Figure I-16: Use sample data to validate a relationship.

You can see from this dataset that a **Pet** can belong to more than one **Breed**, such as Maggie being a German Shepherd/Greyhound mix. You can also see that every **Pet** must belong to at least one **Breed**. We could also have a **Breed** that is not categorizing any **Pets**, such as Chihuahua. In addition, a **Breed** can categorize multiple **Pets**, such as

Joe, Jeff, and Sparky are all Beagles. Answering all six questions leads to a precise relationship. Precise means we all read the model the same exact way.

Let's say there are different answers to our six questions:

Question	Yes	No
Can a Pet belong to more than one Breed?		✓
Can a Breed categorize more than one Pet?	✓	
Can a Pet exist without a Breed?		✓
Can a Breed exist without a Pet?	✓	
Can a Pet be identified without a Breed?	✓	
Can a Breed be identified without a Pet?	✓	

These six answers lead to this model:

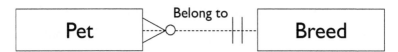

- Each **Pet** must belong to one **Breed**.
- Each **Breed** may categorize many **Pets**.

Figure I-17: Different answers leads to different cardinality.

On this model, we are only including pure-breed pets, as a **Pet** must be assigned one **Breed**. No mutts in our shelter!

We do not capture participation, existence, and identification on Neo4j relationships.

The concept of a relationship exists in Neo4j and it is both similar and different to the concept of a relationship in a traditional data model. It is similar in that a relationship in Neo4j connects two labels. It is different though in what the relationship communicates. In traditional data modeling, the relationship precisely captures the participation, existence, and identification rules.

In Neo4j, the relationship precisely captures the path to navigate from one label to the other. We can communicate the relationship direction and relationship type. Neo4j requires that the application enforce the participation, existence, and identification rules.

Neo4j is a NoSQL database. As such, it cannot enforce the relationship rules that we have just discussed. Although we can model these rules, implementing the rules would be dependent upon the software developers designing our application. For example, Figure I-18 shows our model in Neo4j.

Figure I-18: The relationship in Neo4j.

In Neo4j, the phrase **BELONG_TO** is called a *relationship type*. The relationship type is *FROM* a node *TO* a node. For example, in the model above, the **BELONG_TO** relationship is from the **Pet** to the **Breed.**

In traditional data modeling, we can also have a subtyping relationship. The subtyping relationship groups common entities together. For example, the **Dog** and **Cat** entities might be grouped using subtyping under the more generic **Pet** term. In this example, **Pet** would be called the grouping entity or supertype, and **Dog** and **Cat** would be the terms that are grouped together, also known as the subtypes.

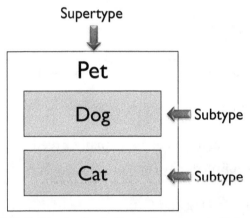

Figure I-19: Subtyping is similar to the concept of inheritance.

We would read this model as:

- Each **Pet** may be either a **Dog** or a **Cat.**
- **Dog** is a **Pet.**
- **Cat** is a **Pet.**

The subtyping relationship means that all of the relationships (and attributes that we'll learn about shortly) that belong to the supertype from other terms also belong to each subtype. Therefore, the relationships to **Pet** also belong to **Dog** and **Cat**. So, for example, cats can be assigned breeds as well, so the relationship to **Breed** can exist at the **Pet** level instead of the **Dog** level, encompassing both cats and dogs. See Figure I-20 for an example.

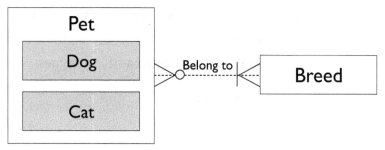

Figure I-20: The relationship to Pet is inherited to Dog and Cat.

So, the relationship:

- Each **Pet** must belong to many **Breeds**.
- Each **Breed** may categorize many **Pets**.

Also applies to **Dog** and **Cat**:

- Each **Dog** must belong to many **Breeds**.
- Each **Breed** may categorize many **Dogs**.
- Each **Cat** must belong to many **Breeds**.
- Each **Breed** may categorize many **Cats**.

Not only does subtyping reduce redundancy, but it also makes it easier to communicate similarities across what would appear to be distinct and separate terms.

If the business logic and requirements dictate it, Neo4j can support subtyping relationships through additional relationship types. The subtyping relationship groups common labels together. For example, the **Dog** and **Cat** labels might be grouped using subtyping under the more generic **Pet** label, as shown in Figure I-21.

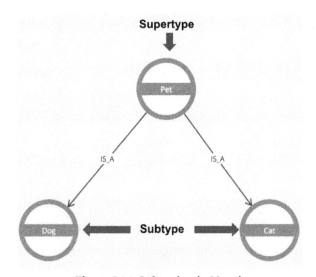

Figure I-21: Subtyping in Neo4j.

- Each **Pet** may be either a **Dog** or a **Cat**.
- **Dog** is a **Pet**.
- **Cat** is a **Pet**.

Unlike other database management systems that you may be familiar with, Neo4j does not support inheritance. That means that a **Cat** or a **Dog** does not inherit all properties of the **Pet**.

In our example, the subtyping relationship **IS_A** allows the user to traverse relationships from the **Cat** or **Dog** node to the **Breed** node. A **Cat IS_A Pet BELONG_TO Breed.** Using the Neo4j cypher language, (:Cat)-[:IS_A]->(:Pet)-[:BELONG_TO]->(:Breed).

Cypher is Neo4j's graph query language that lets you retrieve data from the graph. Cypher is unique because it provides a visual way of matching patterns and relationships. Cypher uses an ASCII-art type of syntax where (nodes)-[:ARE_CONNECTED_TO]->(otherNodes) using rounded brackets for circular (nodes), and -[:ARROWS]-> for relationships. When you write a query, you draw a graph pattern through your data.

There are several great Cypher resources available for you to gain more knowledge on Cypher. They include links from the Neo4j Cypher Manual (https://neo4j.com/developer/cypher/ and https://www.amazon.com/Graph-Data-Processing-Cypher-practical/dp/1804611077/), and the book, *Graph Data Processing with Cypher*.

You now know the additional information a traditional data model provides. Should we build a traditional data model capturing all of the rules, including those of relationships (participation, existence, and identification), when building data models in Neo4j? It is not needed to build a Neo4j database, but would it be worthwhile to build/have the traditional data model to fully understand the nature of the data?

The data model is the foundation for the application. A traditional data model documenting the business rules and data relationships will communicate with consistency and clarity to eliminate guesswork for the developers. When we implement the model in Neo4j, the developer will build the application and add in the logic that maps to the data model.

Attributes (Properties) and keys

On a traditional data model, an entity contains attributes. An *attribute* is an individual piece of information whose values identify, describe, or measure instances of an entity. The entity **Pet** might contain the attributes **Pet Number** that identifies the **Pet**, **Pet Name** that describes the **Pet**, and **Pet Age** that measures the **Pet.**

Attributes take on more precise names when discussing specific technologies. For example, attributes are columns in a RDBMS such as Oracle. Attributes are fields in MongoDB. Attribute are *properties* in Neo4j. In Neo4j, properties are stored as key-value pairs with an individual node or the relationship. A key-value pair is a data type that stores two pieces of related data elements. The first element (key) is a constant used to define the data set. The second element is the value belonging to the data set. For example, a **Pet** may have the following key-value pairs:

- Pet Number: P20230200
- Pet Name: Noodles
- Pet Age: 2

In Neo4j, a label will have a set of properties but each node with that label may have all of the properties or just a subset of the properties. If we want a node to have the property, we will set the property as a not null property. For example, we have a two Pets. We want each Pet to have a Pet Number and a Pet Name property but we don't know one of the pet's age. This would look like the model in Figure I-22.

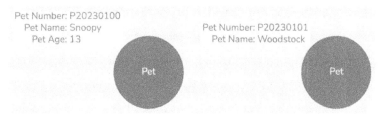

Figure I-22: If we don't know the pet's age for a node, this property will not appear. We do not know Woodstock's age.

In our modeling, we will show all possible properties associated to a label and indicate a property as null or not null. People who are new to graphs and Neo4j often ask when should something be a node or a property. Let's look at our Pet Adoption store for some insights.

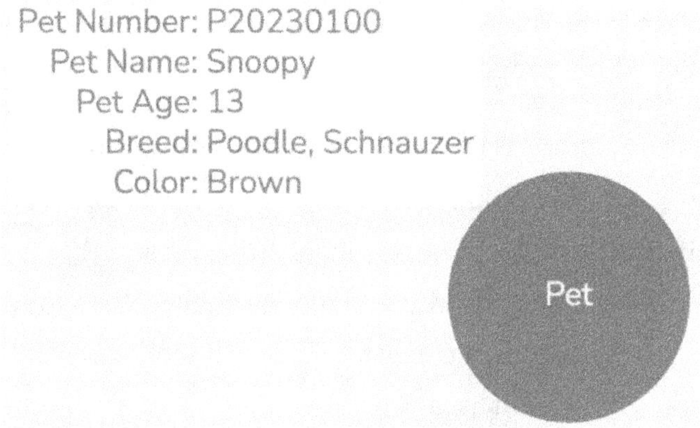

Pet Number: P20230100
Pet Name: Snoopy
Pet Age: 13
Breed: Poodle, Schnauzer
Color: Brown

Figure I-23: When should something be a node or a property?

We could build a model where all of the properties for a **Pet** are on each node. This would be analogous to taking a **Pet** table from a relational database system and mapping each column to a Neo4j property. We may think we are done and that we have a good model, but let's look at some queries.

- Query for all distinct Pet ages
  - MATCH (p:Pet) return distinct 'p.Pet Age';

- Query for all pets named Snoopy
  - MATCH (p:Pet) where 'p.Pet Name' = 'Snoopy' return p;

- Query for all unique Pet Breeds
  - MATCH (p:Pet) return distinct p.Breed;

The first query will find all nodes with the **Pet** label, retrieve the **Pet Age** property and then return the unique values. This query performs well.

The second query will also work well if we have indexed the **Pet Name** property.

The third query will require additional processing as we may have dogs that are multiple breeds. It will take additional work to parse the array and then sort the distinct values. Additionally, there is no guarantee that multiple breeds are stored in a consistent order. It would be complex to find a dog that is a Shih Tzu Bichon mix if someone entered it as Shih Tzu, Bichon. In this case, we would make `Shih Tzu Bichon` a node and create a relationship from the pet to the breed.

Neo4j has the fastest access points on labels, then on relationships, and properties. We will need to remember this as we develop our models.

The advantage of the graph is the fast traversal of relationships. In our use case, we are likely to ask questions similar to the following: "Find me a dog that is either a Shih Tzu Bichon or a Toy Poodle."

Let's look at the model in Figure I-24.

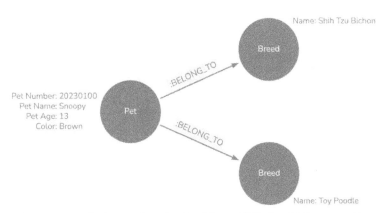

Pet Number: 20230100
Pet Name: Snoopy
Pet Age: 13
Color: Brown

Name: Shih Tzu Bichon

Name: Toy Poodle

Figure I-24: "Find me a dog that is either a Shih Tzu Bichon or a Toy Poodle."

Our query now becomes: **MATCH (p:Pet)-[:BELONG_TO]->(b:Breed) where b.Name IN ['Toy Poodle', 'Shih Tzu Bichon'] return p. 'Pet Name';**

Our query uses an index on the **Breed Name** property to find the breeds that we are interested in and then traverses to the **Pets** and returns the **Pet Name**. This query will perform quickly and is easy to understand.

As we develop our model, our queries will guide us. We want to use the queries to guide our thinking on gaining entry into the graph and running efficient queries. Remember, nodes, labels, and patterns are the best way to access a graph.

You may be thinking, "Why not break all the properties out into their own nodes?" We could have four different nodes for our example **Pet**. See Figure I-25.

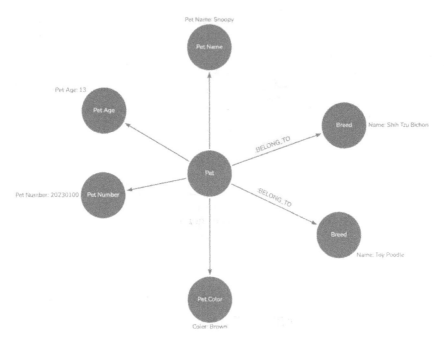

Figure I-25: A node for each property.

This might be an approach if we wanted to find Pets by their name, but how frequently will we search just by name? It might not be that frequent, so let's make that a property. If we wanted to add more metadata about the **Pet Name**, making it a node would allow for more properties. This is a decision that will play into your modeling approach. If you want to return everything about the **Pet**, this requires several relationship traversals and writing OPTIONAL MATCH statements (similar to an outer join) to ensure you retrieve everything about the Pet.

When asked **What should be a Property?**, a guideline would be:

Anything that isn't used as an entry point into the graph, has no complexity / multiplicity (i.e. multiple breeds), and is returned as information about the node is a good candidate for a property.

When modeling in Neo4j, this leads to an iterative process as we adjust the model. There is definitely an art to this, and is something that will become more familiar the more graph models that you develop.

Part of the art of modeling is also knowing how to identify the entity instances. This is where candidate keys add value.

A candidate key is one or more attributes that uniquely identify an entity instance. We assign a **ISBN** (International Standard Book Number) to every title. The **ISBN** uniquely identifies each title and is, therefore, the title's candidate key. **Tax ID** can be a candidate key for an organization in some countries, such as the United States. **Account Code** can be a candidate key for an account. A **VIN** (Vehicle Identification Number) identifies a vehicle.

A candidate key must be unique and mandatory. Unique means a candidate key value must not identify more than one node (or one real-world thing). Mandatory means a candidate key cannot be empty (also known as *nullable*). Each node must be identified by exactly one candidate key value. The number of distinct values of a candidate key is always equal to the number of distinct nodes. If the entity **Title** has **ISBN** as its candidate key, and if there are 500 title instances, there will also be 500 unique ISBNs.

Even though a node may contain more than one candidate key, we can only select one candidate key to be the primary key for a node. A primary key is the candidate key that has been chosen to be *the preferred* unique identifier for an entity. An alternate key is a candidate key that, although it has the properties of being unique and mandatory, was not chosen as the primary key though it may still be used to find specific entity instances.

The primary key appears above the line on a traditional data model, and the alternate key contains the 'AK' in parentheses. So, in the following **Pet** entity, **Pet Number** is the primary key and **Pet Name** is the alternate key. Having an alternate key on **Pet Name** means we cannot have two pets with the same name. See Figure I-26. Whether this can happen or not is a good discussion point. However, the model in its current state would not allow duplicate **Pet Names**.

Figure I-26: An alternate key on Pet Name means we cannot have two pets with the same name.

In Neo4j, the candidate key is called the *node key*. The node key ensures that all nodes with a particular label have a set of defined properties whose combined value is unique and all properties in the set are present.

A candidate key can be either simple, compound, or composite. Table I-2 contains examples of each key type.

	SIMPLE	COMPOUND	COMPOSITE	OVERLOADED
BUSINESS	ISBN	PROMOTION TYPE CODE PROMOTION START DATE	(CUSTOMER FIRST NAME + CUSTOMER LAST NAME + BIRTHDAY)	STUDENT GRADE
SURROGATE	BOOK ID			

Table I-2: Examples of each key type.

Sometimes a single attribute identifies an entity instance, such as **ISBN** for a title. When a single attribute makes up a key, we use the term *simple key*. A simple key can either be a business (also called natural) key or a surrogate key. A business key is visible to the business (such as **Policy Number** for a **Policy**). A surrogate key is never visible to the business. We create a surrogate key to address a technology issue, such as space efficiency, speed, or integration. It is a unique identifier for a table, often a counter, usually fixed-size, and always system-generated without intelligence, so a surrogate key carries no business meaning.

Sometimes it takes more than one attribute to uniquely identify an entity instance. For example, both a **Promotion Type Code** and **Promotion Start Date** may be necessary to identify a promotion. When more than one attribute makes up a key, we use the term *compound key*. Therefore, **Promotion Type Code** and **Promotion Start Date** together are a compound candidate key for a promotion. When a key contains more than one piece of information, we use the term *composite key*. A simple key that includes the customer's first name, last name, and birthday, all in the same attribute, would be an example of a simple composite key. When a key contains different attributes, it is called an *overloaded* key. A **Student Grade** attribute might sometimes contain the actual grade, such as A, B, or C. At other times it might just contain a P for Pass and F for Fail. **Student Grade**, therefore, would be an overloaded attribute. **Student Grade** sometimes contains the student's grade, and other times indicates whether the student has passed the class. Let's look at the model in Figure I-27.

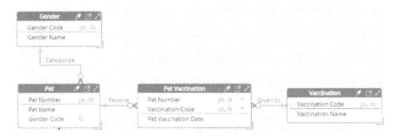

Figure I-27: The entity on the many side contains a foreign key pointing back to the primary key from the entity on the one side.

Here are the rules captured on this model:

- Each **Gender** may categorize many **Pets**.
- Each **Pet** must be categorized by one **Gender**.
- Each **Pet** may Receive many **Vaccinations**.
- Each **Vaccination** may be given to many **Pets**.

The entity on the "one" side of the relationship is called the parent entity, and the entity on the "many" side of the relationship is called the child entity. For example, in the relationship between **Gender** and **Pet**, **Gender** is the parent and **Pet** is the child. When we create a relationship from a parent entity to a child entity, the parent's primary key is copied as a foreign key to the child. You can see the foreign key, **Gender Code**, in the **Pet** entity.

A foreign key is one or more attributes that link to another entity (or, in a case of a recursive relationship where two instances of the same entity may be related, that is, a relationship that starts and ends with the same entity, a link to the same entity). At the physical level, a foreign key allows a relational database management system to navigate from one table to another.

For example, if we need to know the **Gender** of a particular **Pet**, we can use the **Gender Code** foreign key in **Pet** to navigate to the parent **Gender**. In our Neo4j model, we have nodes with the **Pet, Vaccination,** and **Gender** labels. The **GIVEN_TO** relationship has the temporal property of **Vaccination Date**. This simplifies our model and we can identify when a specific vaccination was given to a **Pet**. We can also track multiple vaccinations of the same vaccination code (i.e. Rabies).

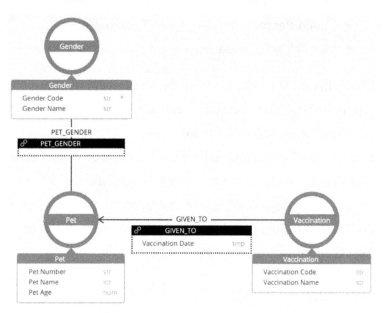

Figure I-28: Foreign keys in Neo4j.

Having **Gender** as a separate node is one of those times when we could store that as a property and use an index to retrieve **Pet(s)** by **Gender**. Each **Pet** has only a single gender and there are likely only two nodes with a **Gender** label. In that case, we could change the model to what appears in Figure I-29.

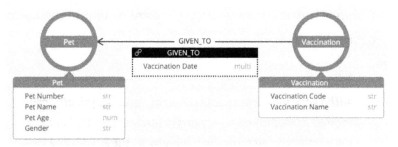

Figure I-29: Simplifying the model.

Three model levels

Traditionally, data modeling produces a set of structures for a Relational Database Management System (RDBMS). First, we build the Conceptual Data Model (CDM) to capture the common business language for the initiative (e.g., "What's a Customer?"). Next, we create the Logical Data Model (LDM) using the BTM's common business language to precisely define the business requirements (e.g., "I need to see the customer's name and address on this report."). Finally, in the Physical Data Model (PDM), we design these business requirements specific for a particular technology such as Oracle, Teradata, or SQL Server (e.g., "Customer Last Name is a variable length required field with a non-unique index..."). Our PDM represents the RDBMS design for an application. We then generate the Data Definition Language (DDL) from the PDM, which we can run within a RDBMS environment to create the set of tables that will store the application's data. To summarize, we go from common business language to business requirements to design to tables.

Although the conceptual, logical, and physical data models have played a very important role in application development over the last 50 years, they will play an even more important role over the next 50 years.

Regardless of the technology, data complexity, or breadth of requirements, there will always be a need for a diagram that captures the business language (conceptual), the business requirements (logical), and the design (physical).

However, the names conceptual, logical, and physical are deeply rooted in the RDBMS side. Therefore, we need to use a more encompassing name for each level to accommodate both RDBMS and NoSQL.

Align = Conceptual, Refine = Logical, Design = Physical

Using the terms Align, Refine, and Design instead of Conceptual, Logical, and Physical has two benefits: greater purpose and broader context.

Greater purpose means that by rebranding into Align, Refine, and Design, we include what the level does in the name. Align is about agreeing on the common business vocabulary so everyone is *aligned* on terminology and general initiative scope. Refine is about capturing the business requirements. That is, refining our knowledge of the initiative to focus on what is important. Design is about the technical requirements. That is, making sure we accommodate the unique needs of software and hardware on our model.

Broader context means there is more than just the models. When we use terms such as conceptual, most project teams only see the model as the deliverable, and do not recognize all of the work that went into producing the model or other related deliverables such as definitions, issue/question resolutions, and lineage (lineage meaning where the data comes from). The align phase includes the conceptual (business terms) model, the refine phase includes the logical model, and the design phase includes the physical model. We don't lose our modeling terms. Instead, we distinguish the model from its broader phase. For example, instead of saying we are in the logical data modeling phase, we say we are in the refine phase, where the logical data model is one of the deliverables. The logical data model exists within the context of the broader refine phase.

However, if you are working with a group of stakeholders who may not warm up to the traditional names of conceptual, logical, and physical, you can call the conceptual the *alignment model*, the logical the *refinement model*, and the physical the *design model*. Use the terms that would have the largest positive impact on your audience.

The conceptual level is Align, the logical Refine, and the physical Design. Align, Refine, and Design—easy to remember and even rhymes!

Business Terms (Align)

We have had many experiences where people who need to speak a common business language do not use the same set of terms consistently. For example, Steve recently facilitated a discussion between a senior business analyst and senior manager at a large insurance company.

The senior manager expressed his frustration on how a business analyst was slowing down the development of his business analytics application. "The team was meeting with the product owner and business users to complete the user stories on insurance quotes for our upcoming analytics application on quotes, when a business analyst asked the question, *What is a quote?* The rest of the meeting was wasted on trying to answer this question. Why couldn't we just focus on getting the Quote Analytics requirements, which we were in that meeting to do? We are supposed to be Agile!"

If there was a lengthy discussion trying to clarify the meaning of a quote, there is a good chance this insurance company does not understand a quote well. It is possible that all business users agree that a quote is an estimate for a policy premium, but disagree at what point an estimate becomes a quote. For example, does an estimate have to be based on a certain percentage of facts before it can be considered a quote?

How well will Quote Analytics meet the user requirements if the users are not clear as to what a *quote* is? Imagine needing to know the answer to this question:

How many life insurance quotes were written last quarter in the northeast?

Without a common alignment and understanding of quote, it is possible for one user to answer this question based on their definition of quote, and someone else can answer based on their different definition of quote. One of these users (or possibly both) will most likely get the wrong answer. Steve has worked with a university whose employees could not come to agreement on what a *student* meant, a manufacturing company whose sales and accounting departments differed on the meaning of *return on total assets*, and a financial company whose analysts battled relentlessly over the meaning of a *trade*—it's all the same challenge we need to overcome, isn't it?

It's about working towards a common business language.

A common business language is a prerequisite for success in any initiative. We can capture and communicate the terms underlying business processes and requirements, enabling people with different backgrounds and roles to understand and communicate with each other.

A Conceptual Data Model (CDM), more appropriately called a Business Terms Model (BTM), is a language of symbols and text that simplifies an informational landscape by providing a precise, minimal, and visual tool scoped for a particular initiative and tailored for a particular audience.

This definition includes the needs of being well-scoped, precise, minimal, and visual. Knowing the type of visual that will have the greatest effectiveness requires knowing the audience for the model.

The audience includes the people who will validate and use the model. Validate means telling us whether the model is correct or needs adjustments. Use means reading and benefiting from the model. The scope encompasses an initiative, such as an application development project or a business intelligence program.

Knowing the audience and scope helps us decide which terms to model, what the terms mean, how the terms relate to each other, and what type of visual would be most effective. Additionally, knowing the scope ensures we don't "boil the ocean" and model every possible term but instead only focus on those that will add value to our current initiative.

Although this model is traditionally called a *conceptual data model*, the term "conceptual" is often not received as a very positive term by those outside the data field. "Conceptual" sounds like a term the IT team would come up with. Therefore, we prefer to call the "conceptual data model" the "business terms model" and will use this term going forward. It is about business terms, and including the term "business" raises its importance as a business-focused deliverable, and also aligns with data governance.

A business terms model often fits nicely on a single piece of paper—and not a plotter-size paper! Limiting a BTM to one page is important because it encourages us to select only key terms. We can fit 20 terms on one page but not 500 terms.

Being well-scoped, precise, minimal, and visual, the BTM provides a common business language. As a result, we can capture and communicate complex and encompassing business processes and requirements, enabling people with different backgrounds and roles to initially discuss and debate terms, and to eventually communicate effectively using these terms.

With more and more data being created and used, combined with intense competition, strict regulations, and rapid-spread social media, the financial, liability, and credibility stakes have never been higher. Therefore, the need for a common business language has never been greater. For example, Figure I-30 contains a BTM for our animal shelter.

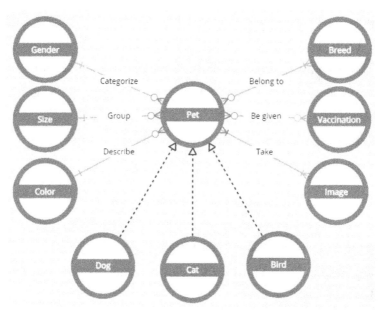

Figure I-30: A business terms model for our animal shelter.

Each of these entities will have a precise and clear definition. For example, **Pet** might have a similar definition to what appears in Wikipedia:

A pet, or companion animal, is an animal kept primarily for a person's company or entertainment rather than as a working animal, livestock, or a laboratory animal.

More than likely, though, there will be something about the definition that provides more meaning to the reader of a particular data model and is more specific to a particular initiative, such as:

A pet is a dog, cat, or bird that has passed all the exams required to secure adoption. For example, if Sparky has passed all of his physical and behavioral exams, we would consider Sparky a pet. However, if Sparky has failed at least one exam, we will label Sparky an animal that we will reevaluate later.

Let's now walk through the relationships:

- Each Pet may be either a Dog, Cat, or Bird.
- Dog is a Pet.
- Cat is a Pet.
- Bird is a Pet.
- Each Gender may categorize many Pets.
- Each Pet must be categorized by one Gender.
- Each Size may group many Pets.
- Each Pet must be grouped by one Size.
- Each Color may describe many Pets.
- Each Pet must be described by one Color.
- Each Pet must belong to many Breeds.
- Each Breed may categorize many Pets.
- Each Pet may be given many Vaccinations.
- Each Vaccination may be given to many Pets.
- Each Pet must take many Images.
- Each Image must be taken of many Pets.

Logical (Refine)

A logical data model (LDM) refines our knowledge of the initiative to focus on what is important, capturing the business requirements without complicating the model with technology concerns. For example, after capturing the common business language for a new order application on a BTM, the LDM will refine this model with attributes and more detailed relationships and entities to capture the requirements for this order application. The BTM would contain definitions for **Order** and **Customer**, and the LDM would contain the **Order** and **Customer** attributes needed to deliver the requirements.

Returning to our animal shelter example, Figure I-31 contains a subset of the traditional logical data model for our animal shelter, and Figure I-32 contains the Neo4j logical data model.

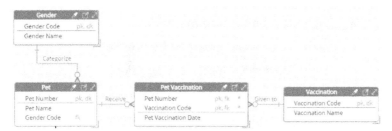

Figure I-31: Logical data model subset for our animal shelter (traditional).

The requirements for our shelter application appear on this model. This model shows the attributes and relationships needed to deliver a solution to the business. For example, in the **Pet** entity, each **Pet** is identified by a **Pet Number** and described by its name and gender. **Gender** and **Vaccination** are defined lists. We also capture that a **Pet** must have one **Gender** and can receive any number (including zero) of **Vaccinations**.

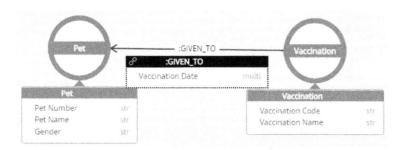

Figure I-32: Logical data model subset for our animal shelter (Neo4j).

In the Graph Model, we eliminated the join table and instead use the relationship **GIVEN_TO** with a Vaccination_Date property to link the **Vaccination** with the **Pet**. We have also moved **Gender** as a property of the **Pet** and will use an index lookup to find a **Pet** that matches the desired **Gender**.

Physical (Design)

The physical data model (PDM) is the logical data model compromised for specific software or hardware. For example, after capturing the common business language for a new order application on a BTM, the LDM will refine this model with attributes and more detailed relationships and entities to capture the requirements for this order application, and the PDM will add technology-specific design considerations to make the application fast and secure. The BTM would contain definitions for **Order** and **Customer**, the LDM would contain the **Order** and **Customer** attributes needed to deliver the requirements, and the PDM would add indexes and other technology-specific components to reduce data retrieval time.

While building the PDM, we address the issues that have to do with specific hardware or software, such as, how can we best design our structures to:

- Process this operational data as quickly as possible?
- Make this information secure?
- Answer these business questions with a sub-second response?

For example, Figure I-33 contains a subset of the physical data model for our animal shelter:

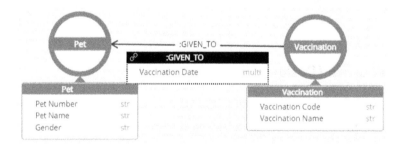

Figure I-33: Physical data model subset for our animal shelter.

We have compromised our logical model to work with specific technology. For example, if we are implementing in a RDBMS such as Oracle, we might need to combine (denormalize) structures together to make retrieval performance acceptable.

As previously mentioned, Neo4j is a NoSQL database. As such, Neo4j cannot define and constrain property lengths and types. Neo4j can enforce null and not null constraints. When using Neo4j, we develop the BTM and the LDM, but enforcing the data types and values are left to the developer and to the application. If it is important to capture the physical data attribute constraints, such as a maximum length or a specific format, using the traditional data model to capture and communicate those details is recommended.

Future versions of Neo4j may include property type constraints (i.e. Pet Age must be an integer) but as of Neo4j 5, those capabilities to not exist.

Three model perspectives

Relational Database Management System (RDBMS) and NoSQL are the two main modeling perspectives. Within the RDBMS, the two settings are relational and dimensional. Within NoSQL, the one setting is query. Therefore, the three modeling perspectives are relational, dimensional, and query.

Table I-3 contrasts relational, dimensional, and query. In this section, we will go into more detail into each of these perspectives.

Factor	Relational	Dimensional	Query
Benefit	Precisely representing data through sets	Precisely representing how data will be analyzed	Precisely representing how data will be received and accessed
Focus	Business rules *constraining* a business process	Business questions *analyzing* a business process	Access paths *providing insights* into a business process
Use case	Operational (OLTP)	Analytics (OLAP)	Discovery
Parent perspective	RDBMS	RDBMS	NoSQL
Example	A Customer must own at least one Account.	How much revenue did we generate in fees by Date, Region, and Product? Also want to see by Month and Year...	Which customers own a checking account that generated over $10,000 in fees this year, own at least one cat, and live within 500 miles of New York City?

Table I-3: Comparing relational, dimensional, and query.

A Relational Database Management System (RDBMS) stores data in sets based on Ted Codd's groundbreaking white papers written from 1969 through 1974. Codd's ideas were implemented in the RDBMS with tables (entities at the physical level) containing attributes. Each table has a primary key and foreign key constraints to enforce the relationships between tables. The RDBMS has been around for so many years primarily because of its ability to retain data integrity by enforcing rules that maintain high-quality data. Secondly, the RDBMS enables efficiency in storing data, reducing redundancy, and saving storage space at the cost of using more CPU power. Over the last decade, the benefit of saving space has diminished as disks get cheaper while CPU performance is not improving. Both trajectories favor NoSQL databases these days.

NoSQL means "NoRDBMS". A NoSQL database stores data differently than a RDBMS. A RDBMS stores data in tables (sets) where primary and foreign keys drive data integrity and navigation. A NoSQL database stores data in files. Although these files can take various forms, such as Resource Description Framework (RDF) triples or Extensible Markup Language (XML), the most common form is JavaScript Object Notation (JSON).

Relational, dimensional, and query can exist at all three model levels, giving us eight different types of models, as shown in Table I-4.

	RELATIONAL	DIMENSIONAL	NoSQL
BUSINESS TERMS (ALIGN)	TERMS AND RULES	TERMS AND PATHS	TERMS AND QUERIES
LOGICAL (REFINE)	SETS	MEASURES WITH CONTEXT	PROPERTY GRAPH MODEL
PHYSICAL (DESIGN)	COMPROMISED SETS	STAR SCHEMA OR SNOWFLAKE	

Table I-4: Eight different types of models.

We discussed the three levels of Align, Refine, and Design in the previous section. We align on a common business language, refine our business requirements, and then design our database. For example, if we are modeling a new claims application for an insurance company, we might create a relational model capturing the business rules within the claims process. The BTM would capture the claims business vocabulary, the LDM would capture the claims business requirements, and the PDM would capture the claims database design.

Relational

Relational models work best when there is a requirement to capture and enforce business rules. For example, a relational may be ideal if an operational application requires applying many business rules, such as an order application ensuring that every order line belongs to one and only one order. The relational perspective focuses on business rules.

We can build a relational at all three levels: business terms, logical, and physical. The relational business terms model contains the common business language for a particular initiative. Relationships capture the business rules between these terms. The relational logical data model includes entities along with their definitions, relationships, and attributes. The relational physical data model includes physical structures such as tables, columns, and constraints. The business terms, logical, and physical data models shared earlier are examples of relational. See Figures I-34, I-35, and I-36.

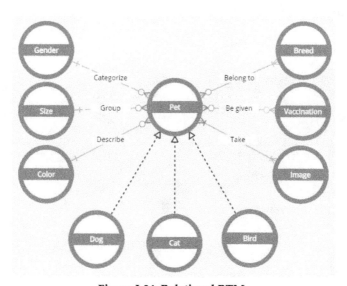

Figure I-34: Relational BTM.

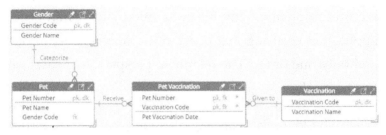

Figure I-35: Relational LDM.

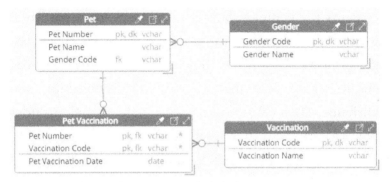

Figure I-36: Relational PDM.

Figure I-37 contains another example of a BTM.

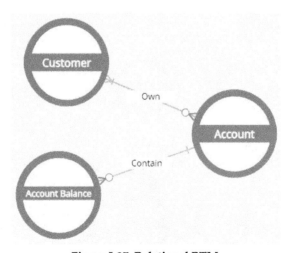

Figure I-37: Relational BTM.

The relationships capture that:

- Each **Customer** may own many **Accounts**.
- Each **Account** must be owned by many **Customers**.
- Each **Account** may contain many **Account Balances**.
- Each **Account Balance** must belong to one **Account**.

We wrote the following definitions during one of our meetings with the project sponsor:

Customer	A customer is a person or organization who has opened one or more accounts with our bank. If members of a household each have their own account, each member of a household is considered a distinct customer. If someone has opened an account and then closed it, they are still considered a customer.
Account	An account is a contractual arrangement by which our bank holds funds on behalf of a customer.
Account Balance	An account balance is a financial record of how much money a customer has in a particular account with our bank at the end of a given time period, such as someone's checking account balance at the end of a month.

For the relational logical data model, we assign attributes to entities (sets) using a set of rules called *normalization*.

Although normalization has a foundation in mathematics (set theory and predicate calculus), we see it more as a technique to design a flexible structure. More specifically, we define normalization as a process of asking business questions, increasing your knowledge of the business and enabling you to build flexible structures that support high-quality data.

The business questions are organized around levels, including First Normal Form (1NF), Second Normal Form (2NF), and Third Normal Form (3NF). These three levels have been neatly summarized by William Kent:

Every attribute depends upon the key, the whole key, and nothing but the key, so help me Codd.

"Every attribute depends upon the key" is 1NF, "the whole key" is 2NF, and "nothing but the key" is 3NF. Note that the higher levels of normalization include the lower levels, so 2NF includes 1NF, and 3NF includes 2NF and 1NF.

To make sure that every attribute depends upon the key (1NF), we need to make sure for a given primary key value, we get at most one value back from each attribute. For example, **Author Name** assigned to a **Book** entity would violate 1NF because for a given book, such as this book, we can have more than author. Therefore, **Author Name** does not belong to the **Book** set (entity) and needs to be moved to a different entity. More than likely, **Author Name** will be assigned to the **Author** entity, and a relationship will exist between **Book** and **Author,** stating among other things, that a **Book** can be written by more than one **Author.**

To make sure every attribute depends upon the whole key (2NF), we need to make sure we have the minimal primary key. For example, if the primary key for **Book** was both **ISBN** and a **Book Title**, we would quickly learn that **Book Title** is not necessary to have in the primary key. An attribute such as **Book Price** would depend directly on the **ISBN,** and therefore including **Book Title** in the primary key would not add any value.

To make sure there are no hidden dependencies ("nothing but the key" which is 3NF), we need to make sure every attribute depends directly on the primary key and nothing else. For example, the attribute **Order Gross Amount** does not depend directly on the primary key of **Order** (most likely, **Order Number**), but instead the components that are used to calculate **Order Gross Amount** (e.g. **List Price** and **Item Quantity**).

Data Modeling Made Simple, by Steve Hoberman, goes more into detail into each of the levels of normalization, including the levels above 3NF. Realize the main purpose of normalization is to correctly organize attributes into sets. Also, note that the normalized model is built according to the properties of the data and not built according to how the data is being used.

Dimensional models are built to answer specific business questions with ease, and NoSQL models are built to answer queries and identify patterns with ease. The relational model is the only model focused on the intrinsic properties of the data and not usage.

Dimensional

A dimensional data model captures the business *questions* behind one or more business processes. The answers to the questions are metrics, such as **Gross Sales Amount** and **Customer Count**.

A dimensional model is a data model whose only purpose is to allow efficient and user-friendly filtering, sorting, and summing of measures. That is, analytics applications. The relationships on a dimensional model represent navigation paths instead of business rules, as with the relational model. The scope of a dimensional model is a collection of related measures plus context that together address some business process. We build dimensional models based upon one or more business questions that evaluate a business process. We parse the business questions into measures and ways of looking at these measures to create the model.

For example, suppose we work for a bank and would like to better understand the fee generation process. In that case, we might ask the business question, "What is the total amount of fees received by **Account Type** (such as Checking or Savings), **Month**, **Customer Category** (such as Individual or Corporate), and **Branch**?" Please see Figure I-38. This model also communicates the requirement to see fees not just at a **Month** level but also at a **Year** level, not just a **Branch** level, but also at a **Region** and **District** level.

Figure I-38: A dimensional BTM for a bank.

Term definitions:

Fee Generation	Fee generation is the business process where money is charged to customers for the privilege to conduct transactions against their account, or money charged based on time intervals such as monthly charges to keep a checking account open that has a low balance.
Branch	A branch is a physical location open for business. Customers visit branches to conduct transactions.
Region	A region is our bank's own definition of dividing a country into smaller pieces for branch assignment or reporting purposes.
District	A district is a grouping of regions used for organizational assignments or reporting purposes. Districts can and often do cross country boundaries, such as North America and Europe districts.
Customer Category	A customer category is a grouping of one or more customers for reporting or organizational purposes. Examples of customer categories are Individual, Corporate, and Joint.
Account Type	An account type is a grouping of one or more accounts for reporting or organizational purposes. Examples of account types are Checking, Savings, and Brokerage.
Year	A year is a period of time containing 365 days, consistent with the Gregorian calendar.
Month	A month is each of the twelve named periods into which a year is divided.

You might encounter terms such as **Year** and **Month** which are commonly understood terms, and therefore minimal time can be invested in writing a definition. Make sure though that these are commonly understood terms, as sometimes even **Year** can have multiple meanings, such as whether the reference is to a fiscal or standard calendar.

Fee Generation is an example of a meter. A meter represents the business process that we need to measure. The meter is so important to the dimensional model that the name of the meter is often the name of the application: the **Sales** meter, the Sales Analytics Application. **District, Region**, and **Branch** represent the levels of detail we can navigate within the **Organization** dimension. A *dimension* is a subject whose purpose is to add meaning to the measures. For example, **Year** and **Month** represent the levels of detail we can navigate within the **Calendar** dimension. So, this model contains four dimensions: **Organization, Calendar, Customer**, and **Account**.

Suppose an organization builds an analytical application to answer questions on how a business process is performing, such as a sales analytics application. Business questions become very important in this case, so we build a dimensional data model. The dimensional perspective focuses on business questions. We can build a dimensional data model at all three levels: business terms, logical, and physical. Figure I-38 displayed our business terms model, Figure I-39 shows the logical, and Figure I-40 the physical.

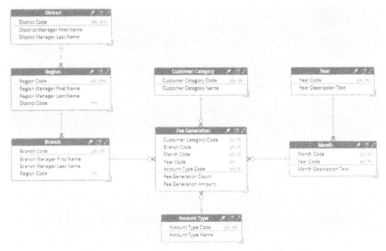

Figure I-39: A dimensional LDM for a bank.

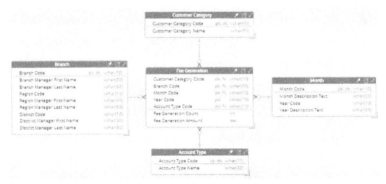

Figure I-40: A dimensional PDM for a bank.

Query

Suppose an organization builds an application to understand their customers in order to solve a problem or predict an outcome. An example might be a customer journey where we want to understand the journey that a patient takes and the treatments they undergo in order to predict a course of treatment. It could be a customer's journey through a website and we want to understand how customers click through the website before leaving the website without a purchase. These types of models are referred to as "event-based" models as the customer wants to derive insights for events. In an event-based model, the pattern of events becomes important so we want to architect the data model to answer pattern-based queries.

We can build a query data model at all three levels: business terms, logical, and physical. Figure I-41 contains a query business terms model, Figure I-42 the query logical data model, and Figure I-41 the query physical data model.

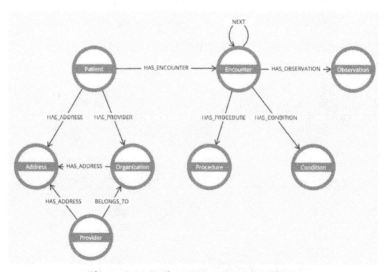

Figure I-41: Patient Journey query BTM.

For a deeper dive into the Patient Journey model, you can refer to this blog post: https://medium.com/neo4j/modeling-patient-journeys-with-neo4j-d0785fbbf5a2.

Great database models help users answer key business questions. Often times, users rely on their past expertise and do not build an efficient data model to answer key business questions. For example, suppose a financial firm wants to understand why their customers are not successful in navigating their website and have to call a customer service agent. According to LiveAgent.com, the industry average cost per contact is $7.16. Our financial firm wants to save money and reduce the number of contacts.

Suppose our financial firm is used to traditional relational data modeling and decides to model the graph data as a simple Customer -> Interaction model. Figure I-42 contains the first attempt at the logical data model.

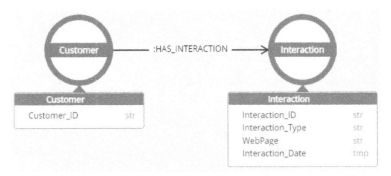

Figure I-42: Patient Journey query LDM, take 1.

This model will be sufficient if our customer wants to know how many interactions a customer has had. It can answer how many interactions of a certain type happened on a certain day or within a date range. However, if we want to look for patterns (Home Page, Account Look Up, Account Application, Service Call), the application will have to retrieve a large amount of data, sort the data, filter the data, and then return the data. It will likely include some recursive queries as well. This works okay for a handful of customers but will not be efficient with millions of customers and events.

This is an "event-based" model where the relationships between the events are the most important part of the data. Neo4j helps us make sense of this data by leveraging these relationships. Our "event-based" model is in Figure I-43.

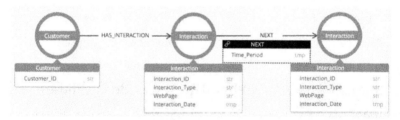

Figure I-43: Patient Journey query LDM, take 2.

Our revised model allows us to find those patterns by writing Cypher queries that ask for those patterns. For example, we can ask questions such as "What four events occurred before a Customer Support Call?" or "What is the average time between types of interactions?" or "What are common patterns this month versus common patterns last month?"

If there are a limited number of Event Types (let's say less than 50), we could model the relationship type as the Event Type and then write queries that find specific patterns. The model would be something like what appears in Figure I-44:

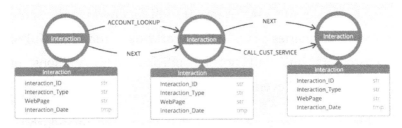

Figure I-44: Patient Journey query LDM, take 3.

This model has both the "NEXT" relationship and the specific relationship types ("ACCOUNT_LOOKUP" and "CALL_CUST_SERVICE"). The "NEXT" relationship can be used to help with graph data science algorithms or machine learning. The specific relationship types can help the user answer event-based queries to identify those event patterns.

It cannot be stated enough that the questions the business wants to answer will drive the queries and the data model. A great graph data model will be able to quickly answer the queries that ask questions about how the relationships between the data. If you try and build a data model without understanding the business use case and questions, you will likely rework the data model.

Additional Neo4j models are available in the Appendix. These models are based on publicly available data or common use cases for a graph database. These data models are meant to be guidelines to help you think about how you could model your use case as a graph.

Recall that when using Neo4j, we develop the BTM and the LDM, but enforcing the data types and values are left to the developer and to the application, and therefore we do not need to distinguish logical from physical in Neo4j.

CHAPTER 1

Align

This chapter will explain the data modeling align phase. We explain the purpose of aligning our business vocabulary, introduce our animal shelter case study, and then walk through the align approach. We end this chapter with three tips and three takeaways.

Purpose

The align stage aims to capture a common business vocabulary for the terms within the initiative. The data model we produce is traditionally called the *conceptual data model (CDM)* or *business terms model (BTM)*. We prefer BTM because it is about business terms. Including the term "business" raises its importance as a deliverable the business users need to be involved in, and *business* aligns more with data governance.

For NoSQL models, we might use a different term than business terms model, such as a *query alignment model*. We also like this term, which is more specific to the purpose of a NoSQL conceptual, as our goal is modeling the queries.

Our animal shelter

A small animal shelter needs our help. They currently advertise their ready-to-adopt pets on their own website. They use a Microsoft Access relational database to keep track of their animals, and they publish this data weekly on their website. See Figure 1-1 for their current process.

A Microsoft Access record is created for each animal after the animal passes a series of intake tests and is deemed ready for adoption. The animal is called a pet once they are ready for adoption.

Figure 1-1. Animal shelter current process.

Once a week, the pet records are updated on the shelter's website. New pets are added and adopted pets have been removed.

Not many people know about this shelter, and, therefore, animals often remain unadopted for much longer than the national average. Consequently, they would like to partner with a group of animal shelters to form a consortium where all of the shelters' pet information will appear on a much more popular website. Our shelter will need to extract data from its current MS Access database and send it to the consortium database in JSON format. The consortium will then load these JSON feeds into their Neo4j database with a web front end.

Let's now look at the shelter's current models. The animal shelter built the business terms model (BTM) in Figure 1-2 to capture the common business language for the initiative.

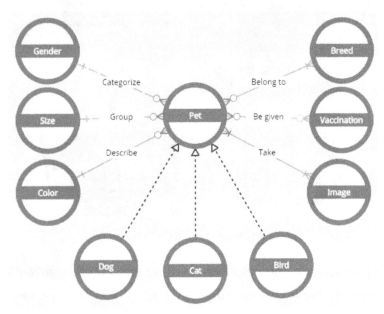

Figure 1-2: Animal shelter BTM.

In addition to this diagram, the BTM also contains precise definitions for each term, such as this definition **Pet** mentioned earlier in the chapter:

A pet is a dog, cat, or bird that has passed all the exams required to secure adoption. For example, if Sparky has passed all of his physical and behavioral exams, we would consider Sparky a pet. However, if Sparky has failed at least one exam, we will label Sparky an animal that we will reevaluate later.

Our animal shelter knows its world well and has built fairly solid models. Recall they will send a subset of their data to a consortium, which the consortium's Neo4j database will receive and load for display on their website. Let's go through the align, refine, and design approach for the consortium as they migrate to a Neo4j database solution.

Approach

The align stage is about developing the initiative's common business vocabulary. We will follow the steps shown in Figure 1-3.

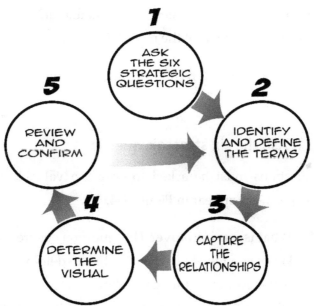

Figure 1-3: Steps to create a BTM.

Before you begin any project, we must ask six strategic questions (Step 1). These questions are a prerequisite to the success of any initiative because they ensure we choose the right terms for our BTM. Next, identify all terms within the scope of the initiative (Step 2). Make sure each term is clearly and completely defined. Then determine how these terms are related to each other (Step 3). Often, you will need to go back to Step 2 at this point because in capturing relationships, you may come up with new terms. Next, determine the most beneficial visual for your audience (Step 4). Consider the visual that would resonate best with those that will need to review and use your BTM. As a final step, seek approval of your BTM (Step 5). Often at this point, there are additional changes to the model, and we cycle through these steps until the model is accepted.

Let's build a relational BTM following these five steps.

Step 1: Ask the six strategic questions

Six questions must be asked to ensure a valuable BTM. These questions appear in Figure 1-4.

1. **What is our initiative?** This question ensures we know enough about the initiative to determine the scope. Knowing the scope allows us to decide which terms should appear on the initiative's BTM. Eric Evans, in his book *Domain-Driven Design*,

introduces the concept of "Bounded Context," which is all about understanding and defining your scope. For example, terms such as **Animal, Shelter Employee,** and **Pet Food** are out of scope.

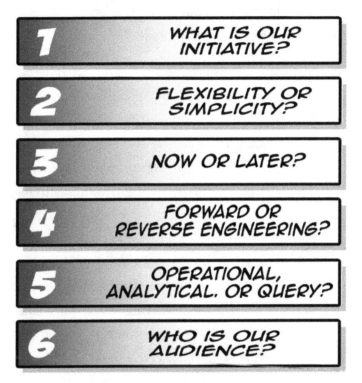

Figure 1-4: Six questions to ensure model success.

2. **Flexibility or simplicity?** This question ensures we introduce generic terms only if there is a need for flexibility. Generic terms allow us to accommodate new types of terms that we do not know about today and also allow us to better group similar terms together. For example, **Person** is flexible and

Employee is simple. **Person** can include other terms we have not yet considered, such as **Adopter, Veterinarian**, and **Volunteer**. However, **Person** can be a more difficult term to relate to than **Employee**. We often describe our processes using business-specific terms like **Employee**.

3. **Now or later?** This question ensures we have chosen the correct time perspective for our BTM. BTMs capture a common business language at a point in time. If we are intent on capturing how business processes work or are analyzed today, then we need to make sure terms, along with their definitions and relationships, reflect a current perspective (now). If we are intent on capturing how business processes work or are analyzed at some point in the future, such as one year or three years into the future, then we need to make sure terms, along with their definitions and relationships, reflect a future perspective (later).

4. **Forward or reverse engineering?** This question ensures we select the most appropriate "language" for the BTM. If business requirements drive the initiative, then it is a forward engineering effort and we choose a business language. It does not matter whether the organization is using SAP or Siebel, the BTM will contain business terms. If an application is driving the initiative, then it is a

reverse engineering effort and we choose an application language. If the application uses the term **Object** for the term **Product**, it will appear as **Object** on the model and be defined according to how the application defines the term, not how the business defines the term. As another example of reverse engineering, you might have as your starting point some type of physical data structure, such as a database layout, an XML, or JSON document. For example, the follow JSON snippet might reveal the importance of **Shelter Volunteer** as a business term:

```
{
  "name": "John Smith",
  "age": 35,
  "address": {
    "street": "123 Main St",
    "city": "Anytown",
    "state": "CA",
    "zip": "12345"
  }
}
```

5. **Operational, analytics, or query?** This question ensures we choose the right type of BTM— relational, dimensional, or query. Each initiative requires its respective BTM.

6. **Who is our audience?** We need to know who will review our model (validator) and who will use our model going forward (users).

1. What is our initiative?

Mary is the animal shelter volunteer responsible for intake. Intake is the process of receiving an animal and preparing the animal for adoption. She has been a volunteer for over ten years, and was the main business resource in building the original Microsoft Access database.

She is enthusiastic about the new initiative, seeing it as a way to get animals adopted in less time. We might start off by interviewing Mary, where the goal is to have a clear understanding of the initiative, including its scope:

> **You**: Thanks for making time to meet with me. This is just our first meeting, and I don't want to keep you behind our allocated time, so let's get right to the purpose of our interview and then a few questions. The earlier we identify our scope and then define the terms within this scope, the greater the chance for success. Can you please share with me more about this initiative?

> **Mary**: Sure! The main driver for our initiative is to make our furry friends get adopted faster. Today on average, our pets are adopted in two weeks. We and other small local shelters would like to get this down to five days on average. Maybe even less, hope so. We will send our pet data to a consortium we have formed with other local shelters to centralize our listings and reach a wider audience.

> **You**: Do you have all types of pets, or just dogs and cats?

Mary: I'm not sure what kinds of pets the other shelters have other than dogs and cats, but we also have birds up for adoption.

You: Ok, and are there any pets to exclude from this initiative?

Mary: Well, it takes a few days for an animal to be assessed to be considered ready for adoption. We run some tests and sometimes procedures. I like to use the term pet when an animal has completed these processes and is now ready for adoption. So, we do have animals that are not yet pets. We are only including pets in this initiative.

You: Got it. And when somebody is looking for a furry best friend, what kinds of filters would they use?

Mary: I've talked with volunteers at the other shelters too. We feel after filtering first on the type of pet, such as dog, cat, or bird, filtering by breed, gender, color, and size would be the most important filters.

You: What kinds of information would someone expect to see when clicking on a pet description that was returned by the filter selections?

Mary: Lots of images, a cute name, maybe information on the pet's color or breed. That sort of thing.

You: Makes sense. What about people? Do you care about people as part of this initiative?

Mary: What do you mean?

You: Well, the people who drop off pets and the people who adopt pets.

Mary: Yes, yes. We keep track of this information. By the way, the people who drop off animals we call surrenderers, and the people who adopt pets are adopters. We are not sending any person details to the consortium. We don't see it relevant and don't want to risk getting sued over privacy issues. Spot the dog will never sue us, but Bob the surrenderer might.

You: I can understand that. Well, I think I understand the scope of the initiative, thank you.

We now have a good understanding of the scope of the initiative. It includes all pets (not all animals) and no people. As we refine the terminology, we might have more questions for Mary around scope.

2. Flexibility or simplicity?

Let's continue the interview to answer the next question.

You: Flexibility or simplicity?

Mary: I don't understand the question.

You: We need to determine whether to use generic terms or, for lack of a better word, more concrete terms. Using generic terms, such as mammal instead of **dog** or **cat,** allows us to accommodate future terms later, such as other kinds of mammals like monkeys or whales.

Mary: We haven't had many whales up for adoption this month. [laughs]

You: Ha!

Mary: Flexibility sounds appealing, but we shouldn't go overboard. I can see eventually we might have other kinds of pets, so a certain level of flexibility would be useful here. But not too much. I remember working on the Microsoft Access system and someone was trying to get us to use a Party concept to capture dogs and cats. It was too hard for us to get our heads around it. Too fuzzy, if you know what I mean.

You: I do know what you mean. Ok, a little flexibility to accommodate different kinds of pets, but not to go overboard. Got it.

3. Now or later?

Now on to the next question.

You: Should our model reflect how things are now at the shelter or how you would like it to be after the consortium's application is live?

Mary: I don't think it matters. We are not changing anything with the new system. A pet is a pet.

You: Ok, that makes things easy.

As we can see from our conversations on these first three questions, getting to the answers is rarely straightforward and easy. However, it is much more efficient to ask them at the beginning of the initiative instead of making assumptions early on and having to perform rework later, when changes are time-consuming and expensive.

4. Forward or reverse engineering?

Since we first need to understand how the business works before implementing a software solution, this is a forward engineering project, and we will choose the forward engineering option. This means driven by requirements and, therefore, our terms will be business terms instead of application terms.

5. Operational, analytics, or query?

Since this initiative is about displaying pet information to drive pet adoption, which is query, we will build a query BTM.

6. Who is our audience?

That is, who is going to validate the model and who is going to use it going forward? Mary seems like the best candidate to be the validator. She knows the existing application and processes very well and is vested in ensuring the new initiative succeeds. Potential adopters will be the users of the system.

Step 2: Identify and define the terms

We first focus on the user stories, then determine the detailed queries for each story, and finally sequence these queries in the order they occur. It can be iterative. For example, we might identify the sequence between two queries and realize that a query in the middle is missing that will require modifying or adding a user story. Let's go through each of these three steps.

1. Write user stories

User stories have been around for a long time and are extremely useful for NoSQL modeling. Wikipedia defines a user story as: *...an informal, natural language description of features of a software system.* The user story provides the scope and overview for the BTM, also known as a query alignment model. A query alignment model accommodates one or more user stories. The purpose of a user story is to capture at a very high level how an initiative will deliver business value. User stories take the structure of the template in Figure 1-5.

TEMPLATE	COVERS
AS A (STAKEHOLDER)	WHO?
I WANT TO (REQUIREMENT)	WHAT?
SO THAT (MOTIVATION)	WHY?

Figure 1-5: User story template.

Here are some examples of user stories from tech.gsa.gov:

- As a Content Owner, I want to be able to create product content so that I can provide information and market to customers.

- As an Editor, I want to review content before it is published so that I can ensure it is optimized with correct grammar and tone.

- As a HR Manager, I need to view a candidate's status so that I can manage their application process throughout the recruiting phases.

- As a Marketing Data Analyst, I need to run the Salesforce and Google analytics reports so that I can build the monthly media campaign plans.

To keep our animal shelter example relatively simple, assume our animal shelter and others that are part of the consortium met and determined these are the most popular user stories:

1. As a potential dog adopter, I want to find a particular breed, color, size, and gender, so that I get the type of dog I am looking for. I want to ensure that the dog's vaccinations are up to date.

2. As a potential bird adopter, I want to find a particular breed and color so that I get the bird I am looking for.

3. As a potential cat adopter, I want to find a particular color and gender, so that I get the type of cat I am looking for.

2. Capture queries

Next, we capture the queries for the one or more user stories within our initiative's scope. While we want to capture multiple user stories to ensure we have a firm grasp of the scope, having just a single user story that drives a NoSQL application is ok. A query starts off with a "verb" and is an action to do something. Some NoSQL database vendors use the phrase "access pattern" instead of query. We will use the term "query" to also encompass "access pattern".

Here are the queries that satisfy our three user stories:

Q1: Only show pets available for adoption.

Q2: Search available dogs by breed, color, size, and gender that have up-to-date vaccinations.

Q3: Search available birds by breed and color.

Q4: Search available cats by color and gender.

Now that we have direction, we can work with the business experts to identify and define the terms within the initiative's scope.

Recall our definition of a term as a noun that represents a collection of business data and is considered both basic and critical to your audience for a particular initiative. A term can fit into one of six categories: who, what, when, where, why, or how. We can use these six categories to create a terms template for capturing the terms on our relational BTM. See Figure 1-6.

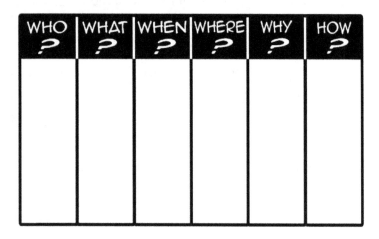

Figure 1-6: Terms template.

This is a handy brainstorming tool. There is no significance to the numbers. That is, a term written next to #1 is not meant to be more important than a term written next to #2. In addition, you can have more than five terms in a given column, or in some cases, no terms in a given column.

We meet again with Mary and came up with this completed template in Figure 1-7, based on our queries.

WHO?	WHAT?	WHEN?	WHERE?	WHY?	HOW?
SURRENDERER	PET	VACCINATION DATE	CRATE	VACCINATE	VACCINATION
ADOPTER	DOG			ADOPT	ADOPTION
	CAT			PROMOTE	PROMOTION
	BIRD				
	BREED				
	GENDER				
	COLOR				
	SIZE				
	IMAGE				

Figure 1-7: Initially completed template for our animal shelter.

Notice that this is a brainstorming session, and terms might appear on this template but not on the relational BTM. Those terms that will be excluded fit into three categories:

- **Too detailed**. Several concepts on this template appear to be attributes and, therefore, will appear on the logical data model and not the BTM. For example, **Vaccination Date** is more detailed than **Pet** and **Breed**.

- **Out of scope**. Brainstorming is a great way to test the scope of the initiative. Often, terms added to the terms template require additional discussions to determine whether they are in scope. For example, terms such as **Surrenderer** and **Adopter** we know are out of scope for the animal shelter's initiative.

- **Redundancies**. Why and How can be very similar. For example, the event **Vaccinate** is documented by the **Vaccination**. The event **Adopt** is documented by **Adoption**. Therefore, we may not need both the event and documentation. In this case, we choose the documentation. That is, the How instead of the Why.

After taking a lunch break, we met again with Mary and refined our terms template, as shown in Figure 1-8.

WHO ?	WHAT ?	WHEN ?	WHERE ?	WHY ?	HOW ?
~~SURRENDERER~~	PET	~~VACCINATION DATE~~	~~CRATE~~	~~VACCINATE~~	VACCINATION
~~ADOPTER~~	DOG			~~ADOPT~~	~~ADOPTION~~
	CAT			~~PROMOTE~~	~~PROMOTION~~
	BIRD				
	BREED				
	GENDER				
	COLOR				
	SIZE				
	IMAGE				

Figure 1-8: Refined template for our animal shelter.

We might have a lot of questions during this brainstorming session. It is a great idea to ask questions as they come up. There are three benefits of raising questions:

- **Become known as the detective.** Become comfortable with the level of detective work needed to arrive at a precise set of terms. Look for holes in the definition where ambiguity can sneak in, and ask questions the answers to which will remove this ambiguity and make the definition precise. Consider the question, "Can a pet be of more than one breed?" The answer to this question will refine how the consortium views pets, breeds, and their relationship.

- **Uncover hidden terms**. Often the answers to questions lead to more terms on our BTM—terms that we might have missed otherwise. For example, better understanding the relationship between **Vaccination** and **Pet** might lead to more terms on our BTM.

- **Better now than later**. The resulting BTM offers a lot of value, yet the process of getting to that final model is also valuable. Debates and questions challenge people, make them rethink and, in some cases, defend their perspectives. If questions are not raised and answered during the process of building the BTM, the questions will be raised and need to be addressed later on in the lifecycle of the initiative, often in the form of data and process surprises, when changes are time-consuming and expensive. Even simple questions like "Are there other attributes that we could use to describe a pet?" can lead to a healthy debate resulting in a more precise BTM.

Here are definitions for each term:

Pet	A dog, cat, or bird that is ready and available to be adopted. An animal becomes a pet after they have passed certain exams administered by our shelter staff.
Gender	The biological sex of the pet. There are three values that we use at the shelter: • Male • Female • Unknown The unknown value is used when we are not sure of the gender.
Size	The size is most relevant for dogs, and there are three values that we assign at the shelter: • Small • Medium • Large Cats and birds are assigned medium, except for kittens which are assigned small and parrots which are assigned large.
Color	The primary shade of the pet's fur, feathers, or coat. Examples of colors include brown, red, gold, cream, and black. If a pet has multiple colors, we either assign a primary color or assign a more general term to encompass multiple colors, such as textured, spotted, or patched.
Breed	From Wikipedia, because this definition applies to our initiative: *A breed is a specific group of domestic animals having homogeneous appearance, homogeneous behavior, and/or other characteristics that distinguish it from other organisms of the same species.*

Vaccination	A shot given to a pet to protect it from disease. Examples of vaccinations are rabies for dogs and cats, and polyomavirus vaccine for birds.
Image	A photograph taken of the pet that will be posted on the website.
Dog	From Wikipedia, because this definition applies to our initiative: *The dog is a domesticated descendant of the wolf. Also called the domestic dog, it is derived from the extinct Pleistocene wolf, and the modern wolf is the dog's nearest living relative. Dogs were the first species to be domesticated by hunter-gatherers over 15,000 years ago before the development of agriculture.*
Cat	From Wikipedia, because this definition applies to our initiative: *The cat is a domestic species of small carnivorous mammal. It is the only domesticated species in the family Felidae and is commonly referred to as the domestic cat or house cat to distinguish it from the wild members of the family.*
Bird	From Wikipedia, because this definition applies to our initiative: *Birds are a group of warm-blooded vertebrates constituting the class Aves, characterized by feathers, toothless beaked jaws, the laying of hard-shelled eggs, a high metabolic rate, a four-chambered heart, and a strong yet lightweight skeleton.*

Step 3: Capture the relationships

Even though this is a query BTM, we can ask the Participation and Existence questions to precisely display the business rules for each relationship. Participation questions determine whether there is a one or a many symbol on the relationship line next to each term. Existence questions determine whether there is a zero (may) or one (must) symbol on the relationship line next to either term.

Working with Mary, we identify these relationships on the model:

- **Pet** can be a **Bird, Cat,** or **Dog.** (Subtyping)
- **Pet** and **Image.**
- **Pet** and **Breed.**
- **Pet** and **Gender.**
- **Pet** and **Color.**
- **Pet** and **Vaccination.**
- **Pet** and **Size.**

Table 1-1 contains the answers to the Participation and Existence questions for each of these seven relationships (excluding the subtyping relationship).

Question	Yes	No
Can a Gender categorize more than one Pet?	✓	
Can a Pet be categorized by more than one Gender?		✓
Can a Gender exist without a Pet?	✓	
Can a Pet exist without a Gender?		✓
Can a Size categorize more than one Pet?	✓	
Can a Pet be categorized by more than one Size?		✓
Can a Size exist without a Pet?	✓	
Can a Pet exist without a Size?		✓
Can a Pet be described by more than one Color?		✓
Can a Color describe more than one Pet?	✓	
Can a Pet exist without a Color?		✓
Can a Color exist without a Pet?	✓	
Can a Pet be described by more than one Breed?	✓	
Can a Breed describe more than one Pet?	✓	
Can a Pet exist without a Breed?		✓
Can a Breed exist without a Pet?	✓	
Can a Pet be given more than one Vaccination?	✓	
Can a Vaccination be given to more than one Pet?	✓	
Can a Pet exist without a Vaccination?	✓	
Can a Vaccination exist without a Pet?	✓	
Can a Pet take more than one Image?	✓	
Can an Image be taken of more than one Pet?	✓	
Can a Pet exist without an Image?		✓
Can an Image exist without a Pet?		✓

Table 1-1. Answers to the Participation and Existence questions.

After translating the answers to each of these questions into the model, we have our animal shelter BTM. See Figure 1-9.

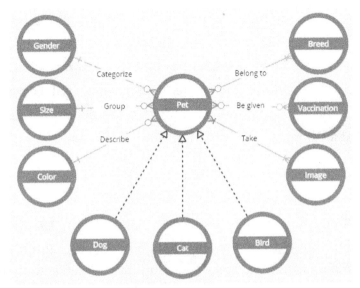

Figure 1-9: Our animal shelter BTM (showing rules).

These relationships are read as:

- Each **Gender** may categorize many **Pets**.
- Each **Pet** must be categorized by one **Gender**.
- Each **Size** may group many **Pets**.
- Each **Pet** must be grouped by one **Size**.
- Each **Color** may describe many **Pets**.
- Each **Pet** must be described by one **Color**.
- Each **Pet** must belong to many **Breeds**.
- Each **Breed** may be assigned to many **Pets**.
- Each **Pet** may be given many **Vaccinations**.
- Each **Vaccination** may be given to many **Pets**.
- Each **Pet** must take many **Images**.
- Each **Image** must be taken of many **Pets**.
- Each **Pet** may either be a **Dog, Cat,** or **Bird**.
- **Dog** is a **Pet**. **Cat** is a **Pet**. **Bird** is a **Pet**.

The answers to the participation and existence questions are context-dependent. That is, the scope of the initiative determines the answers. In this case, because our scope is the subset of the animal shelter's business that will be used as part of this consortium's project, we know at this point that a **Pet** must be described by only one **Color**.

We determined, though, that a Neo4j database should be used to answer these queries. You can see how the traditional data model provides value in terms of making us ask the right questions and then providing a powerful communication medium showing the terms and their business rules. Even if we are not implementing our solution in a relational database, this BTM provides value.

Build a relational data model even though the solution is in a NoSQL database such as Neo4j, if you feel there can be value. That is, if you feel there is value in explaining the terms with precision along with their business rules, build the relational BTM. If you feel there is value in organizing the attributes into sets using normalization, build the relational LDM. It will help you organize your thoughts and provide you with a very effective communication tool. Be flexible on the visual as well. If showing entities as circles instead of rectangles resonate better with your audience, use circles.

Our end goal, though, is to create a Neo4j database. Therefore, we need a query BTM. So, we need to determine the order someone would run the queries.

Graphing the sequence of queries leads to the query BTM. The query BTM is a numbered list of all queries necessary to deliver the user stories within the initiative's scope. The model also shows a sequence or dependency among the queries. The query BTM for our five queries would look like what appears in Figure 1-10.

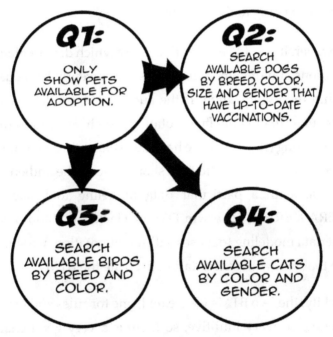

Figure 1-10: Our animal shelter BTM (showing queries).

All of the queries depend on the first query. That is, we first need to filter by animal type.

Step 4: Determine the visual

Someone will need to review your work and use your model as input for future deliverables such as software development, so deciding on the most useful visual is an important step. After getting an answer to Strategic Question #4, *Who is our audience?*, we know that Mary will be our validator.

There are many different ways of displaying the BTM. Factors include the technical competence of the audience and the existing tools environment.

However, it would be helpful to know which data modeling notations and data modeling tools are currently being used within the organization. If the audience is familiar with a particular data modeling notation—such as Information Engineering (IE), which we have been using throughout this book—that is the notation we should use. If the audience is familiar with a particular data modeling tool, such as IDERA's ER/Studio, erwin DM, or Hackolade Studio, and that data modeling tool uses a different notation, we should use that tool with that notation to create the BTM.

Luckily, the two BTMs we created, one for rules and one for queries, are very intuitive, so there is a very good chance our models will be well-understood by the audience.

Step 5: Review and confirm

Previously we identified the person or group responsible for validating the model. Now we need to show them the model and make sure it is correct. Often at this stage, after reviewing the model, we make some changes and then show them the model again. This iterative cycle continues until the model is agreed upon by the validator and approved.

Three tips

1. **Organization**. The steps you went through in building this "model" are the same steps we go through in building any model. It is all about organizing information. Data modelers are fantastic organizers. We take the chaotic real world and show it in a precise form, creating powerful communication tools.

2. **80/20 Rule.** Don't go for perfection. Too many requirements meetings end with unfulfilled goals by spending too much time discussing a minute particular issue. After a few minutes of discussion, if you feel the issue's discussion may take up too much time and not lead to a resolution, document the issue and keep going. You will find that for modeling to work well with Agile and other iterative approaches, you may have to forego perfection and sometimes even

completion. Much better to document the unanswered questions and issues and keep going. Much better to deliver something imperfect yet still very valuable than deliver nothing. You will find that you can get the data model about 80% complete in 20% of the time. One of your deliverables will be a document containing unanswered questions and unresolved issues. Once all of these issues and questions are resolved, which will take about 80% of your time to complete, the model will be 100% complete.

3. **Diplomat.** As William Kent said in **Data and Reality** (1978), *so, once again, if we are going to have a database about books, before we can know what one representative stands for, we had better have a consensus among all users as to what "one book" is.* Invest time trying to get consensus on terms before building a solution. Imagine someone querying on pets within having a clear definition as to what a pet is.

Three takeaways

1. Six strategic questions must be asked before you begin any project (Step 1). These questions are a prerequisite to the success of any initiative because they ensure we choose the right terms for our BTM. Next, identify all terms within the scope of the initiative (Step 2). Make

sure each term is clearly and completely defined. Then determine how these terms are related (Step 3). Often, you will need to go back to Step 2 at this point, because in capturing relationships, you may come up with new terms. Next, determine the most beneficial visual for your audience (Step 4). Consider the visual that would resonate best with those needing to review and use your BTM. As a final step, seek approval of your BTM (Step 5). Often at this point, there are additional changes to the model, and we cycle through these steps until the model is accepted.

2. Understand the business problem. Ask yourself if this is a graph problem. Are the relationships between data elements providing high value or not? Are there several depths of relationship? If so, then a graph database is a good solution and you have to model the domain as a graph model. Don't try and model a graph problem using other database modeling techniques.

3. As organized data modelers, be consistent in the naming conventions. Relationship types should be descriptive and should describe the relationship. Everything should not be "RELATED_TO". We would not model **PET RELATED_TO BREED** and **PET RELATED_TO CAT**.

CHAPTER 2

Refine

This chapter will explain the data modeling refine phase. We explain the purpose of refine, refine the model for our animal shelter case study, and then walk through the refine approach. We end the chapter with three tips and three takeaways.

Purpose

The purpose of the refinement stage is to create the logical data model (LDM) based on our common business vocabulary defined during the align stage. Refine is how the modeler captures the business requirements without complicating the model with implementation concerns, such as software and hardware.

The shelter's Logical Data Model (LDM) uses the common business language from the BTM to precisely define the business requirements. The LDM is fully-attributed yet independent of technology. We build the relational LDM by normalizing, covered in Chapter 1. Figure 2-1 contains the shelter's relational LDM.

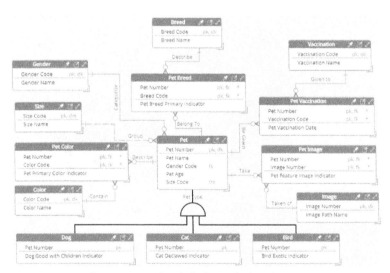

Figure 2-1: Animal shelter relational LDM.

Neo4j is a NoSQL database which means it is schemaless. As a data modeler, we expect our tools to eventually generate a DDL that we can apply as part of the physical data model.

Since Neo4j is schemaless, we often fall into the trap of modeling data instead of building a data model.

Our goal is to build a data model that is based on the user requirements.

When we say "modeling data", we mean that we may get a spreadsheet of 100 rows describing an animal shelter. Instead of modeling for a **Pet,** we may model for the pet Rover. If Rover is a single breed, we may miss the fact that a pet can have multiple breeds. If Rover has only had a single vaccination, we may model the vaccination as a property of the **Pet** node instead as a separate node.

It is important to use the sample data to validate the data model instead of using the sample data as the data model. Business rules or relationships may be missed if we model the data.

As we build out our LDM, we realize that modeling for a RDBMS and Neo4j are similar. However, we need to be aware of some important differences:

- In Neo4j, a node can have multiple labels versus only a single table in a relational database. That is, in Neo4j, an instance can belong to more than one entity.

- There can be multiple relationships between two distinct nodes versus a primary key / foreign key relationship.

- Relationships between nodes with the same label are crucial, which is less common in the RDBMS world.

- RDMBS often store multiple properties. Neo4j excels at relationships and less so with many properties on a node. A general rule would be to limit the number of properties to around 20 per node. While this is a general rule, there are times when you will need to exceed that rule and have more than 20 properties on a node. With that in mind, we need to be precise on what properties to place on a node. We should only store properties in Neo4j that are used to query on or filter against. Extraneous properties take up storage space and may impact query performance. However, if you do need the properties to display to the end users, you may store them with the understanding of potential storage and query impact.

- When we need to relate multiple items together, Neo4j will use an intermediate node to ensure that we properly model the relationships and present accurate data. For example, if the animal shelter wanted to track veterinary visits, we would introduce an **Event** node that would connect the pet, the veterinarian, veterinarian clinic, and vaccination(s). This would look something like the model in Figure 2-2.

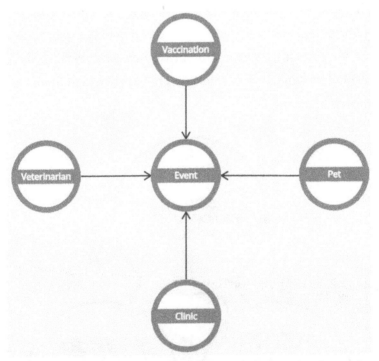

Figure 2-2. The event node links the Pet, Clinic, Veterinarian, and Vaccination together. We can easily tell which clinic and which veterinarian gave which vaccination to a pet.

The shelter's Logical Data Model (LDM) uses the common business language from the BTM to precisely define the business requirements (e.g., "I need to see the customer's name and address on this report."). The LDM is fully attributed and defines the implementation of the system, yet independent of technology.

Approach

The refine stage is all about determining the business requirements for the initiative. The end goal is a logical data model which captures the attributes and relationships needed to answer the queries. The steps to complete are shown in Figure 2-3.

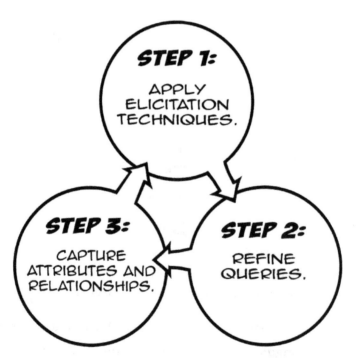

Figure 2-3: Refinement steps.

Similar to determining the more detailed structures in a traditional logical data model, we determine the more detailed structures needed to deliver the queries during the refinement stage. You can therefore call the query LDM a query refinement model if you prefer. The query refinement model is all about discovery and captures the answers to the queries that reveal insights into a business process.

The graph model is highly conducive to eliciting and capturing the important questions that drive the queries. In addition, this model is easy to understand and allows the end users to quickly understand what data is available and how data relates to other data.

Step 1: Apply elicitation techniques

This is where we interact with the business stakeholders to identify the attributes and relationships needed to answer the queries. We keep refining, usually until we run out of time. Techniques we can use include interviewing, artifact analysis (studying existing or proposed business or technical documents), job shadowing (watching someone work), and prototyping. You can use any combination of these techniques to obtain the attributes and relationships to answer the queries. Often these techniques are used within an Agile framework. You choose which techniques to use based on your starting point and the needs of the stakeholders. For example, if a stakeholder says, "I don't know what I want, but I'll know when I see it," building a prototype would be the best approach. Frequently, and especially for Neo4j, in situations where we don't know what questions are even possible to answer, we start with artifact analysis by first studying an existing data set.

Elicitation must drive out the use cases and knowing the end-users of the graph. An optimal schema design will depend on the users and the use case that these users will be addressing. To drive towards an optimal design, the elicitation phase should ask questions such as:

- Who will be the users of the graph?
- What types of questions will the users ask?
- What data does the user need access?
- What are the queries that will be written to answer the user's questions?

The answers you receive during the elicitation will determine how to create an effective database design. The data model and the use case must stay in-step.

Step 2: Refine queries

The refinement process is iterative, and we keep refining, again, usually until we run out of time. Ideally, we develop queries that answer the business questions.

Step 3: Capture attributes and relationships

Ideally, we want to identify the most important queries. These queries impact the business and, therefore, the business will pay to implement these. We review our logical model to identify the attributes and relationships needed for each of the queries identified in the query refinement model.

In this stage, we should document the naming convention or styles for our Entities (Nodes), Attributes (Properties) and Relationships. In Neo4j, each of these items are case sensitive meaning that **PET** is a different entity from **Pet.** A consistent style guide will ensure that the data is consistent and we do not introduce unexpected items into our database. A good starting point is the Neo4j style guide.[3]

Using artifact analysis, we can start with the animal shelter's logical, and use this model as a good way to capture the attributes and relationships within our scope.

Based on the queries, quite a few of our concepts are not directly needed for search or filtering, and so they can become additional descriptive attributes on the **Pet** entity. For example, the pet shelter wants to know what vaccinations a pet has received and when that vaccination occurred. See Figure 2-4.

---

[3] https://neo4j.com/developer/cypher/style-guide/.

This model still allows us to capture multiple vaccinations given to a single pet. When we query the database, we can sort the results by the **Vaccination Date** to show the order of vaccinations for a specific pet. We could also query the database to identify the number of pets with a specific vaccination.

Figure 2-4: The graph model for queries on vaccinations.

Figure 2-5 contains the complete graph LDM.

This model has been developed based on the business requirements and the expected queries. This model does not change based on various queries and, therefore, can be used as the starting point model for all queries.

Let's briefly walk through the model. The shelter identifies each **Pet** with a **Pet Number**, which is a unique counter assigned to the **Pet** the day the **Pet** arrives. Also entered at this time is the pet's name (**Pet Name**) and age (**Pet Age Quantity**). If the **Pet** does not have a name, it is given one by the shelter employee entering the pet's information, who is careful not to assign the same name as another pet currently available for adoption. If the age is unknown, it is estimated by the shelter employee entering the pet's information.

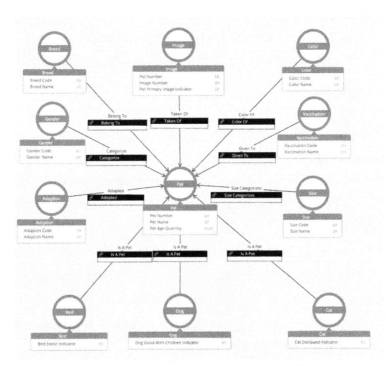

Figure 2-5: Animal shelter complete graph LDM.

If the **Pet** is a **Dog**, the shelter employee entering the information performs a few assessments to determine whether the dog is good with children (**Dog Good With Children Indicator**). If the **Pet** is a **Cat**, the shelter employee determines whether the **Cat** has been declawed (**Cat Declawed Indicator**). If the **Pet** is a **Bird**, the shelter employee enters whether it is an exotic bird such as a parrot (**Bird Exotic Indicator**).

Notice two patterns on the model. The first is the use of decode entities. **Gender, Adoption, Size, Vaccination, Breed,** and **Color** all provide a lookup structure with a code and decode (e.g. 'B' is for the color 'Brown' and 'L' is for the size 'Large'). The second is the many-to-many relationship pattern. A **Pet** can be assigned more than one **Breed,** be administered more than one **Vaccination,** contain more than one **Color,** and take more than one **Image.** The featured image for the **Pet** on the website is the image where **Pet Featured Indicator** equals 'Y'. The primary breed for the **Pet** is the assigned breed where **Pet Breed Primary Indicator** equals 'Y'. The primary color for the **Pet** is the assigned color where **Pet Primary Color Indicator** equals 'Y'. These two patterns also show that there is no need to maintain a foreign key on the **Pet** node. The relationships indicate the relationships between the **Pet** and the **Featured Indicator** or the **Vaccination.**

The Neo4j model is a straight-forward approach. You may hear the term "Tables to Labels" which means that the customary RDBMS tables are assigned a label, the columns (fields) on the relational tables become node properties in the graph, and the join tables are transformed into relationships with the columns on the join tables becoming relationship properties.

With Neo4j, you do not need to worry about table joins and index lookups because graph data is structured by each, individual entity and its relationships with other individual entities. Neo4j allows users to model their data to address their specific requirements. In the example we discussed, we modeled the data in a more traditional transactional and reporting model. We can ask questions about a specific pet or about a specific vaccination. Imagine if we now wanted to look at the pet data to see if there are patterns in how the pets are treated. For people, we would call this the patient journey. For our pets, let's call it Pet Journey.

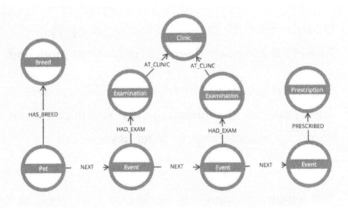

Figure 2-6: Animal shelter complete graph LDM.

This data model is an "event-driven" model where we focus on a series of events to understand a pet's journey. When we model events, we look at the actions of individual pets. Over the course of time, an individual pet would participate in a number of events.

While one pet may be interesting, the collection of pet journeys could be very interesting. For example, we may begin to see a pattern where a pet has multiple examinations before a medication is prescribed, or we may see a pattern in prescribing a series of medications. Event-based modeling also makes it easier for us to pick out "outliers," individuals exhibiting unusual behavior. We can also begin to group individuals based on having similar behavior patterns.

Three tips

1. Queries will define how you model your graph. Identify the top user queries to drive your modeling.

2. Step back and ensure that you are building a data model and not just modeling data. You may miss an edge case, relationship, or other key piece of information.

3. Use a logical naming convention for your labels, nodes, and relationships.

Three takeaways

1. Building a graph model is different from building a RDMBS model. Know the differences and leverage the graph advantages. Don't model a graph in the same manner as an RDMBS implementation.

2. Graph models are not usually resolved and finalized in the first iteration. It is normal for multiple iterations before we finalize on the model.

3. Don't be afraid to experiment with different data models as you are working to understand the user requirements.

CHAPTER 3

Design

This chapter will explain the data modeling design phase. We explain the purpose of design, design the model for our animal shelter case study, and then walk through the design approach. We end the chapter with three tips and three takeaways.

Purpose

The purpose of the design stage is to create the physical data model (PDM) based on the business requirements defined in our logical data model. Design is how the modeler captures the technical requirements without compromising the business requirements, yet accommodating the initiative's software and technology needs for the initiative.

The design stage is also where we accommodate history. That is, we modify our structures to capture how data changes over time. For example, the Design stage would allow us to keep track of not just the most recent name for a pet, but also the original. For example, the animal shelter changes a pet's name from Sparky to Daisy. Our design could store the original pet name and the most current, so we would know Daisy's original name was Sparky. Although this is not a book on temporal data or modeling approaches that gracefully allow for storing high data volatility or varying history requirements, such as the Data Vault,[4] you would need to consider such factors in the Design stage.

Data modelers and other users who are familiar with PDMs from other databases may expect that that they will be able to define a property type and size. For example, the **Pet**

---

[4] For more on the data vault, read John Giles' *The Elephant in the Fridge*.

Name must be a VARCHAR of length 30 or the **Pet Number** must be an Integer. Neo4j does not support specifying a property type or size. Neo4j does support NOT NULL and UNIQUE constraints. This means that the data typing and size must be handled at the application layer and/or during the data extraction, transformation, and loading (ETL) phase.

Figure 3-1 contains the Physical Data Model (PDM) representing the animal shelter's Neo4j database design.

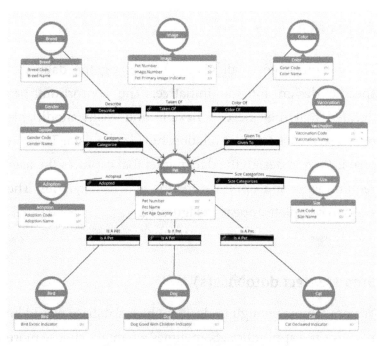

Figure 3-1: PDM of animal shelter.

We have added in the desired data types and the nullability. Remember that Neo4j can only support null/not null property values. This model aligns with our logical data model in that we are showing the relationships between nodes and communicating the desired label names and relationship types. This model hasn't denormalized any of the relationships as the queries will still be performant and we don't want to impose any artificial constraints on the users. For example, we don't want to limit the number of a pet's photographs or vaccinations.

Approach

The design stage is all about developing the database-specific design for the initiative. The consortium has decided that they need a flexible and easily modifiable database focused on the relationships in the data. The end goal is then to design the data model that captures the user requirements and optimize for the end user queries. The steps to complete appear in Figure 3-2.

Step 1: Select database(s)

We now know enough to decide which database would be ideal for the application. Sometimes we might choose more than one database if we feel it would be the best architecture for the application. We know in the consortium's case that they have selected Neo4j because of the value in the relationships and that they wanted a database that can easily adapt to new requirements.

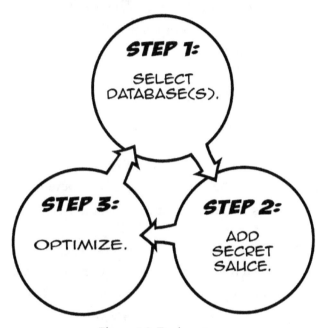

Figure 3-2: Design steps.

Step 2: Add secret sauce

Although the NoSQL databases are very similar, each database has something special to consider during design. Neo4j is designed to leverage the relationships in the data and allows users to rapidly traverse those relationships to find the answers to their questions.

In Neo4j, we store the relationships between the nodes and relationships. While we pay the penalty for creating the *joins* at load time, we gain the performance during query time by not having to join data. We simply do lookups to find the next node or relationship. This applies to graphs of a few thousand nodes to graphs of billions of nodes. Let's dive into this a little more.

In relational databases, references to other rows and tables are indicated by referring to primary key attributes via foreign key columns. Joins are computed at query time by matching primary and foreign keys of all rows in the connected tables. These operations are compute-heavy and memory-intensive and have an exponential cost.

When many-to-many relationships occur in the model, you must introduce a JOIN table (or associative entity table) that holds foreign keys of both the participating tables, further increasing join operation costs. Figure 3-3 shows this concept of connecting a **Pet** (from the **Pet** table) to a **Breed** (in the **Breed** table) by creating a **Pet_To_Breed** join table that contains the **ID** of the pet in one column and the **ID** of the associated breed in the next column.

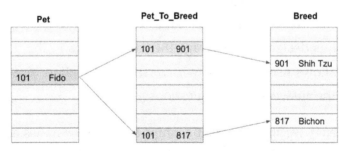

Figure 3-3: Introducing a join table.

As you can probably see, this makes understanding the connections very cumbersome because you must know the **Pet ID** and **Breed ID** values (performing additional lookups to find them) to know which person connects to which departments. Those types of costly join operations are often addressed by denormalizing the data to reduce the number of joins necessary, therefore breaking the data integrity of a relational database.

Contrast that to the implementation in Neo4j. Each node in Neo4j directly and physically contains a list of relationship records that represent the relationships to other nodes. These relationship records are organized by relationship type and direction (incoming or outgoing) and may hold additional attributes. Whenever you run the equivalent of a JOIN operation, the graph database uses this list, directly accessing the connected nodes and eliminating the need for expensive search-and-match computations. See Figure 3-4.

Neo4j is flexible and consistent—you can add data, nodes, and properties during run time. For example, if the animal shelter decided to allow the adopting of **SNAKE**s, the application could create a new node with the LABEL SNAKE as part of a query. This is different from a relational database where the **SNAKE** table would be created with a DDL statement.

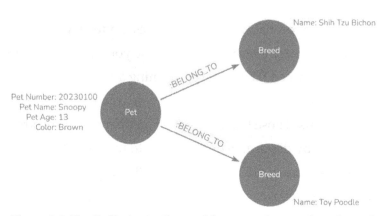

Figure 3-4: Neo4j eliminates the need for expensive search-and-match computations.

Neo4j will just store the data as whatever you give it. It's schema-optional in that way, as we have discussed. If the user entered the **Pet Id** as a string instead of an integer, Neo4j would accept this data as a string and not report a data type violation. If a user added a new property (venomous), Neo4j would add that new property to the node. This is powerful, but it does place the responsibility on the user to ensure consistency in the data types as they are entered into Neo4j.

Step 3: Optimize

Similar to indexing, denormalizing, partitioning, and adding views to a RDBMS physical model, we would add database-specific features to the query refinement model to produce the query design model (also called the *physical data model*).

Designing a graph model is often described as part art and part science. People new to Neo4j often ask when an item should be a node and when it should be a property.

"Is it a node, a relationship, or a property?" This question breaks things down into the smallest units that Neo4j utilizes. Even though we have discussed these components earlier, we can still be flexible when defining something as a node and a property. This is less rigid and less defined as opposed to many relational models.

The answer to this question depends on the types of queries that we want to run against Neo4j. Remember that we need to discover the types of queries that users want to run during the elicitation phase. With that in mind, Neo4j accesses nodes by labels the fastest, then by relationships, and finally on properties. A good model supports the queries that it needs to run with the best performance.

When you think of how you will query your data, think of the data elements that drive access into your graph. Nodes, labels, and pattern matches using the relationships are the best way to access a graph. The ability to identify a starting point for your query will be the driving force for performance. Identifying that entry point should be one of the main factors in deciding how to model the graph.

If you think back to our animal shelter model, we *could* create a single node called **Pet** and attach multiple properties to that node for everything from the photos to the vaccinations to the breed. We could easily find all of the **Pets,** but any filtering or comparison by property or combination of properties will be painful. This might address one query, but our overall performance will suffer.

Properties are the slowest access point for Neo4j. We want to be careful and judicious on when and how to use properties. We *could* place the **Vaccination Date** on the **Vaccination** node. This would create a unique node for an individual **Pet** and their individual **Vaccination.** However, if we want to find **Pets** who had the same **Vaccination** within a date range, we would place the **Vaccination Date** on the relationship type between the **Pet** and the **Vaccination.** We will index that relationship property which will help us find all **Pets** with that **Vaccination** within a date range.

Tip: Neo4j supports a limited set of property types. Be aware of the available property types, which may affect your physical design.

Nodes are often the primary entry into the graph. As such, some people ask, "Shouldn't we have all the properties as a node?" In this case, we will ask ourselves, "Will we use this node to access the graph, is there a complexity / multiplicity to this object, and/or do we need to return this value with other node values back to the user?" If yes, these are examples of properties that should remain as a property.

For example, we normally would not split out an **Address** into multiple nodes. We would keep the **Address Line 1** along with the **City** and the **State/Province** together on a node. Most users would not want to find "901 M Street" across the entire graph. Likewise, in our adoption model, the **Pet** is likely to be a single **Gender**. We can move the **Gender** node to a property, index the property, and use the indexed property to assist the user during the query.

Breed is a good example of a property best modeled as a Node. A pet may consist of multiple breeds and we want users to find a pet that is of one or more breeds. We would not want to store this as a list or an array inside of Neo4j because users may misspell a breed, or the list of breeds is stored in a different order for each pet making searching and comparing a difficult problem. To make this easier, we use **Breed** as a node with a relationship to the **Pet.**

Three tips

1. Nodes and labels are the best way to access a graph when querying and representing distinct entities.

2. Relationships are powerful ways to access different types of nodes at the same time, move through the graph, and filter data. Yet relationship properties can be difficult to utilize for other logic (such as attempting to find equality among different relationships).

3. Properties are suited for data that isn't a point of access directly, can't be broken down further or duplicated, and/or needs to be considered a component of a node.

Three takeaways

1. Always keep the users in mind. The graph model must assist them in answering their business questions.

2. Create multiple graphs for different use cases. An optimized graph for a specific use case will perform much better than an all-encompassing graph.

3. In Neo4j, the logical data model is implemented as the physical data model when data is added to the database. The developer is responsible for implementing any constraints or defined data types in the application layer.

Appendix

We have included different data models for different use cases as a starting point for your graph journey.

Fraud detection

Traditional fraud prevention measures focus on discrete data points such as specific accounts, individuals, devices, or IP addresses. However, today's sophisticated fraudsters escape detection by forming fraud rings comprised of stolen and synthetic identities. To uncover such fraud rings, it is essential to look beyond individual data points to the connections that link them. The fraud detection data model links the Suspect / Customer with their identities and allows a user to quickly identify shared identifiers and leverage graph data science algorithms to quickly identify communities.

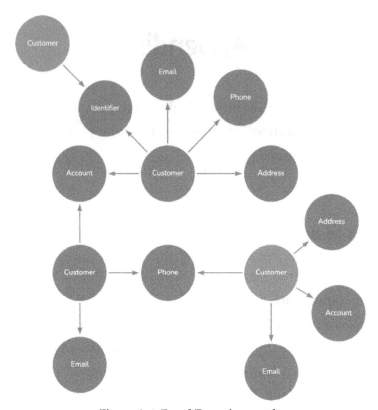

Figure A-1: Fraud Detection graph.

Figure A-2: Fraud Detection schema.

Real time recommendations

Consumers expect relevant recommendations and businesses strive to provide recommendations that will entice a customer to spend money. With graph technology, you are able to combine a customer's browsing behavior and demographics with their buying history to instantly analyze their current choices and immediately provide relevant recommendations – all before a potential customer clicks to a competitor's website.

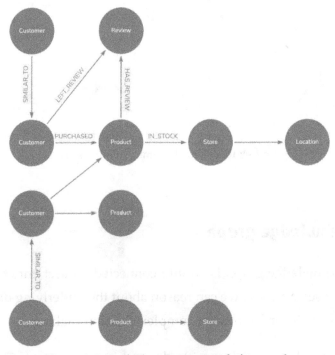

Figure A-3: Real-Time Recommendation graph.

Purchase history, feedback, and shopping cart interactions can be linked together to drive meaningful insight. Whether the business wants to recommend an item of interest to an individual or whether the business wants to identify individuals for a given product or set of products, storing these relationships in a graph database will allow for businesses to serve up the most relevant results for each question.

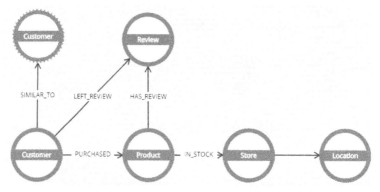

Figure A-4: Real-Time Recommendation schema.

Knowledge graph

A knowledge graph is an interconnected dataset enriched with semantics so we can reason about the underlying data and use it confidently for complex decision-making.

Knowledge graphs provide deep, dynamic context. They enable people to find all related information in one place, with all of the relationships across that data. As you add more information, knowledge graphs become increasingly valuable. The following diagram is an example of a Geospatial Knowledge Graph.

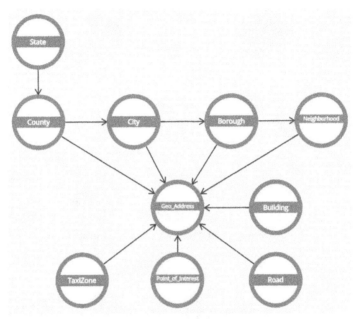

Figure A-5: Knowledge Graph schema.

Anti-money laundering

Anti-money laundering teams at financial services firms are using Neo4j to model companies, accounts, and transactions as a graph to discover instances of money laundering. By graphing the relationships between all of these entities, AML teams can track how and where funds are moving through automated Cypher queries that map to traditional money laundering behaviors. Once a suspicious transfer of funds occurs, the system can automatically flag the transaction for review by an AML analyst.

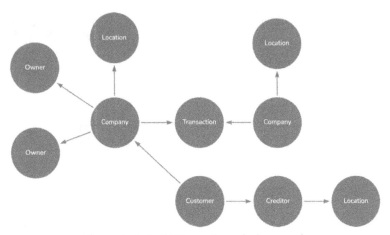

Figure A-6: Anti-Money Laundering graph.

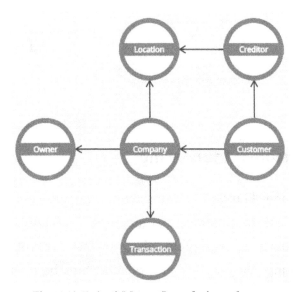

Figure A-7: Anti-Money Laundering schema.

Master data management

Businesses use master data. It's often held in many different places, with lots of overlap and redundancy, in different formats, and with varying degrees of quality. Master Data Management (MDM) is the practice of identifying, cleaning, storing, and – most importantly – governing this data.

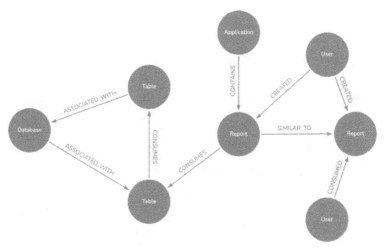

Figure A-8: Master Data Management graph.

Because MDM data is highly connected, changing, and not often shared, a graph database can make modeling this data much easier than other database solutions. By creating an MDM system referencing the other systems of record, your MDM solution easily connects these siloed data systems (accounting, inventory, sales, CRM).

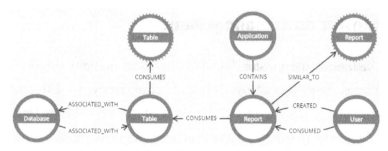

Figure A-9: Master Data Management schema.

Supply chain management

Supply chains are often a complex network with multiple relationships between suppliers, warehouses, transportation and eventually the consumers. When something goes wrong (produce recall), consumers want to have greater transparency into the supply chain.

Similarly, when there are potential disruptions to a company's vendors, the company wants to understand where the points of failure are as well as alternatives. Businesses are digitizing their supply chains to better visualize and understand who they are working with:

- Where are they located?
- Who are their suppliers?
- What is our failure points?

Figure A-10: Supply Chain Management graph.

Given the length and complexity of modern supply chains, most of these data relationships are not hierarchical or one-to-one, but rather interconnected and involving multiple levels.

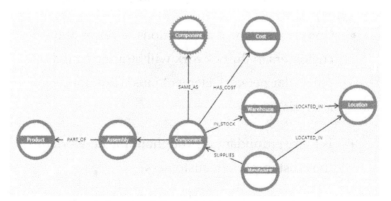

Figure A-11: Supply Chain Management schema.

Network and IT

As with master data, a graph database is used to bring together information from disparate inventory systems, providing a single view of the network and its consumers – from the smallest network element all the way to the applications, services and customers who use them.

A graph representation of a network enables IT managers to catalog assets, visualize their deployment and identify the dependencies between the two. The graph's connected structure enables network managers to conduct sophisticated impact analyses, answering questions like:

- Which parts of the network – applications, services, virtual machines, physical machines, data centers, routers, switches and fiber – do particular customers depend on? (Top-down analysis)

- Conversely, which applications, services and customers in the network will be affected if a particular network element fails? (Bottom-up analysis)

- Is there redundancy throughout the network for the most important customers?

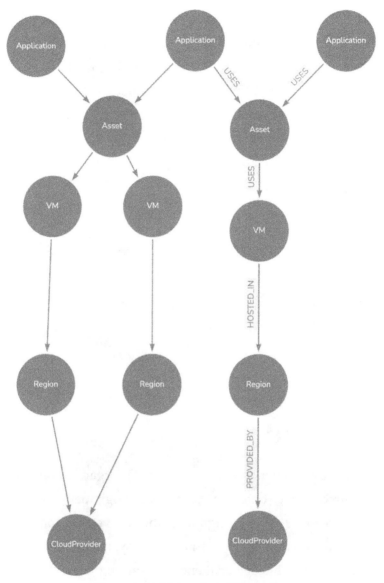

Figure A-12: Network and IT graph.

A graph database representation of the network can also enrich operational intelligence based on event correlations.

Whenever an event correlation engine (such as a Complex Event Processor) infers a complex event from a stream of low-level network events, it assesses the impact of that event against the graph model and triggers any necessary compensating or mitigating actions.

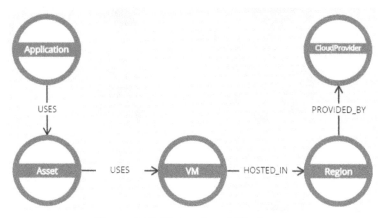

Figure A-13: Network and IT schema.

Data lineage

Banks and other regulated financial organizations are required to trace data dependencies through many intricate levels before reaching original, authoritative data sources – a crucial underlying requirement most systems simply can't address. Data lineage challenges stemming from stringent requirements like BCBS 239 require a lot more flexibility and persistence than traditional data storage systems offer.

Often financial institutions are required to backwards trace data through discrete data silos until its lineage ends with an authoritative source. Likewise, even though entities require standard identifiers, business groups often use their own terminology and algorithms – sometimes within the same organization.

The structure and location of data often make it all but impossible to address in a single, centralized data store. And ironically, moving everything into a single repository may make tracing data lineage even more difficult.

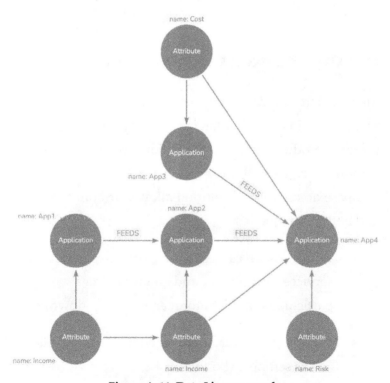

Figure A-14: Data Lineage graph.

Integrating information into a single, enterprise-wide logical data model requires graph technology. With a graph database, you get a single source of truth and complex or hidden data connections are queried and revealed within milliseconds.

Figure A-15: Data Lineage schema.

Identity and access management

Identity and Access Management hierarchies can often be represented in a graph. Managing multiple changing roles, groups, products and authorizations is an increasingly complex task. As with network and IT operations, a graph database access control solution allows for both top-down and bottom-up queries:

- Which resources – company structures, products, services, agreements, and end users can a particular administrator manage? (Top-down)

- Given a particular resource, who can modify its access settings? (Bottom-up)

- Which resource can an end-user access?

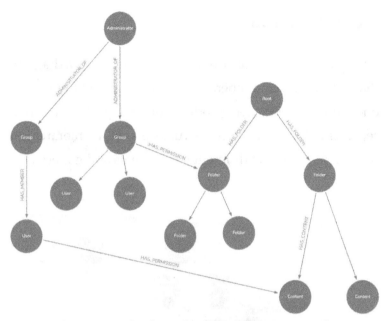

Figure A-16: Identity and Access Management graph.

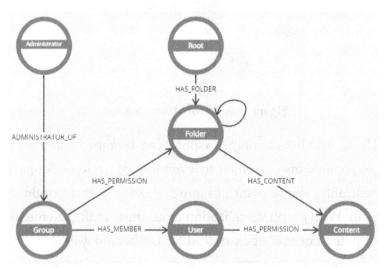

Figure A-17: Identity and Access Management schema.

Bill of Materials

"A Bill of Material (BoM), or product structure, is a diagram that lists all the components and parts required to produce one unit of a finished product, or end part. It is often represented as a tree structure with hierarchical relationships among different components and materials."

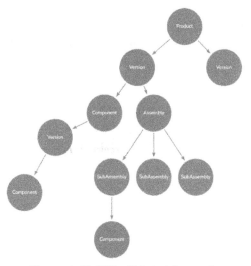

Figure A-18: Bill of Materials graph.

Using graph technology, a BoM can be represented as a graph allowing customers to leverage graph queries for part centrality, single point of failure, shortest path or optimal path. With graph visualization tools, these critical elements or paths can easily be surfaced for further analysis.

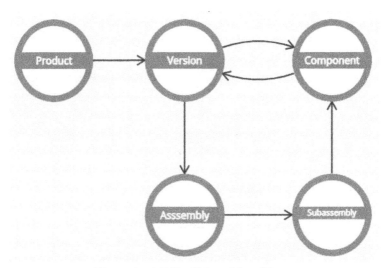

Figure A-19: Bill of Materials schema.

A deeper look at using graphs for BoM can be found here: https://journals.sagepub.com/doi/10.1177/184797901773263 8.

Index

www.ingramcontent.com/pod-product-compliance
Lightning Source LLC
Chambersburg PA
CBHW071249050326
40690CB00011B/2314